Finding Your Capital **S** Story

Why your Story Drives your Brand

Paul Furiga
President • Chief Storyteller
WordWrite

Cover and Interior Design: Rachel Booth / RelyOn Creative
Illustrations: Emily Marko
Author Photo: Adam Michaels Photography
Book Editor: Bonnie Budzowski / Gravitas Press

"Bubblebath Teapot" story © 2020 by Damion Searls: used by permission

CONTENTS

CHAPTER	TITLE	PAGE
	Acknowledgements	i
	Foreword	iii
	Introduction: Why there are "stories" and there are "Stories"	v
1	What's biology got to do with marketing? Storytelling isn't bull crap, it's biology	1
2	Our Brains: Hardwired for story, hungry for meaning	19
3	What's wrong in marketing today? The squandered legacy of John Wanamaker	45
4	Uncovering YOUR great untold story	67
5	The WordWrite story: How I got here	89
6	How to uncover your Capital S Story with StoryCrafting	107
7	If you're selling to B2B or B2C, do you share your story differently?	133
8	Storytelling and social media: Made for each other	155
9	Beware the storytelling charlatans	173
10	Just do it: Your Capital S Story can drive your success	189
	About the Author	201
	How to work with WordWrite	203

ACKNOWLEDGMENTS

As you'll see in the pages to come, I take a long view of the definition of story. Chapter after chapter, our lives and careers unfold with unpredictable twists and turns that take us places we could never have imagined.

This is my way of promising two things: One, I won't make this into a book in itself. Two, hard as I try, I will forget many people, so my apologies in advance. For those of you who don't find your name, please know you have contributed to my story, often in ways that you might be surprised to learn.

Every story has at least one hero. Mine has many, starting with the life partner who's been with me nearly all the way, my beautiful wife Brenda. Our daughters Emily and Elizabeth have also been great heroes and storytelling teachers as the chapters of their lives have unfolded. Our families have been great contributors too, starting with my father, a World War II storyteller whose adventures I will share in a future book.

I've had two or three careers, depending upon how you count them, and many of those who helped me along the way get their just due in the chapters ahead. So, let me say thanks to all those whose lessons aren't shared later:

Thank you to the teachers, including George Masterson and George Belden, who taught me to be curious. Thank you to my editors and colleagues, who taught me the meaning of story, including Ellen Stein Burbach, Joe Duffus, Sue Gorisek, David Hawkings, David Lowery, Dick Maloy, Bob Mitchell, Pete Roper, Bill Sternberg, Randy Wynn and so many others.

Thank you to principled public servants, including the late U.S. Sen. Paul Simon, who taught me that very public stories can be authentic as well as compelling and engaging.

WordWrite and our StoryCrafting℠ methodology are now well established, so the list of WordWriters who've contributed to the jewels in this book is long. Among the many we've been blessed to have on our team, these fine storytellers stand out:

Megan King, our very first "employee;" Tara LaPinto Darazio, our first full-time employee; and so many others: Logan Armstrong, Hollie Geitner, Emma Walter Gielata, Erin O'Connor Hogan, Keira Koscumb, Shannon Baker Meyer, Robin Rectenwald, Dan Stefano, Deanna Ferrari Tomaselli and Samantha Wannemacher.

A special thanks to fellow travelers on the storytelling journey who've made the roller coaster experience of a real-life story worth the travel: John Durante, who over more than a decade has helped develop the application of StoryCrafting; Jeremy Church, my business partner, who's done so much to bring StoryCrafting to life internally and with clients; and Dick Singer, my business and VISTAGE coach for more than a dozen years.

Finally, a special thanks to those very smart people around me who've kept me on the right track: trusting clients and friends including Eric Guy of the Center for Victory and Dave McClintock and the entire McClintock & Associates team; collaborators including Bonnie Budzowski of Gravitas Press, who helped me get this book over the finish line, Rachel Booth of RelyOn Creative, who's tolerated innumerable goofy requests from me in designing this book, my illustrator Emily Marko, who's brought our concepts to life with wit and style in the coming pages; and members of VISTAGE CE Group 676 who've poked, prodded, questioned and championed the ideas in the book and the book itself from beginning to end.

Paul Furiga
Pittsburgh, PA
November 2020

FOREWORD

"Well, it's about time!" Those were the words I said to Paul Furiga almost 20 years ago when he announced that he was starting his own public relations business. We were at a weekly breakfast in which four unemployed former executives would meet to help and hold each other accountable in our job search.

Paul went on to start his firm and grow it into the success it has become. He started in a spare bedroom in his house, eventually moving into an office suite near the house and then to a larger suite in downtown Pittsburgh, and now in a beautiful newly redone office suite in the Alcoa Building downtown.

Through those years, I've watched and, I'm proud to say, been a part of a story of determination, courage, and firm belief in himself and his colleagues to create an organization that truly understands that every company and every person has a story. As his VISTAGE Chair, I've watched as Paul's business grew and, more importantly, as Paul has grown into a true CEO. One characteristic of a true CEO is the knowledge that there is always more to learn. Paul has never lost that curiosity to explore new perspectives. He has won his VISTAGE group's Most Valuable Player award at least three times and is a strong contributor when it comes to helping his fellow members with their issues and bringing his own issues to the group.

Together with his wife Brenda and their two daughters, Emily and Elizabeth, Paul Furiga has proven day in and day out that "nice guys" don't have to finish last.

Reading this book will teach you what storytelling is all about and will give you more insight into your own story. An opportunity to learn from the master.

Dick Singer
Best Practice Chair, VISTAGE
Pittsburgh 2020

INTRODUCTION

WHY THERE ARE "STORIES" AND THERE ARE "**STORIES**"

The Sunday, February 6, 2011 front page of the *Detroit Free Press* carried this teaser for a business story inside the paper, "Colleges retool training to get auto engineers back to work."

Across the Motor City that day, ice fog and a weak sun reflected the bleak, below-freezing temperatures that could have described the American auto industry as well as it did the weather.

On that Sunday, the auto industry was still staggering from the ferocious hit it took in the financial collapse of 2008. Though the federal government had stepped in with loans and a controversial $80.7 billion bailout package for General Motors and Chrysler, critics continued to question the long-term future of American car making.

GM and Chrysler had declared bankruptcy in 2009 and shed billions in debt. And American auto factories, while capable of making 17 million cars, produced only 10 million in 2010. Hundreds of thousands of autoworkers lost their jobs.

By the end of 2010, the worst seemed to be over. American automakers could start thinking about life beyond a bailout. The so-called Big Three U.S. automakers—Chrysler, Ford and GM—envisioned a resurrection of their image—and fortunes. This meant giving their attention (and wallets) to the savants who had shaped the glamour and glitter of American car ownership since the end of World War II: the advertising industry.

That's why, on February 6, 2011, nearly 1,200 miles from bleak Detroit in sunny Arlington, Texas, one of the historic leaders in the auto industry hung its hopes on a two-minute TV commercial that would air during the Super Bowl that day. Even for those who hated football, the Super Bowl sporting event had become the Super Bowl advertising event, a cultural touchstone of entertainment and humor and curiosity stuffed between the tackles and touchdowns. In any given year, the Super Bowl was watched by more human beings than any other live television event, many of them tuning in only for the ads.

Over the decades, American car making and American ad making had fed off each other, the nation's largest consumer industry fueling America's largest creative industry. The result had been a mutual admiration society in which vivid imagery, music and cars drove what many observers considered the quintessential definition of American culture. As one 1974 ad put it, "Baseball, hot dogs, apple pie and Chevrolet, they go together in the good ol' USA."

So it was only natural that, with the auto bailout providing stability and breathing room, Chrysler invested $12.4 million to produce what is still considered the most expensive ad in history, a "we're back" homage to Detroit dubbed "Born of Fire."

The spot, with gritty, iconic images of the Motor City, paired Detroit's history of metal-banging car making with the musical strains of hometown rapper Eminem. The soundtrack featured an instrumental version of Eminem's first number 1 hit, *Lose Yourself,* from his semi-autobiographical film about growing up in Detroit, *8 Mile.*

As the music thumped in the background and narrator Kevin Yon provided commentary challenging the idea that Detroit was dead, Eminem tooled through town behind the wheel of a sleek, black sedan, with his face only partially lit by passing street-lights on a dark, rainy night.

Eminem's journey ended at the Fox Theatre, a 1920s gem that is a symbol of Detroit's 20th-century status as a cultural as well as car-making capital. As Eminem entered the 5,000-seat, cavernous national historic landmark, *The Selected of God*, an African-American gospel choir, seamlessly merged their voices with the thump of *Lose Yourself* until Eminem reached the stage. Then they hushed their voices to hold long, low tones as Eminem turned to the camera and said, "This is the Motor City, and this is what we do."

With that, images of the new Chrysler 200 sedan flashed across the screen, and finally, an in-your-face tagline, "Imported from Detroit." Boom!

As art and as emotional statement, the ad was a huge hit. National media credited it with giving hope to Detroiters and with restoring faith in American manufacturing.

Initially, the business press and trade media were ecstatic over the marriage of auto making and advertising.

In naming the internal Chrysler team as "Marketer of the Year," Ad Age celebrated work that "Restored Motor City Pride in a Bankrupt Chrysler With Campaigns That Resonated Across America and Lifted Sales an Astounding 37%."

Basking in the glow, Chrysler's top marketing executive, Olivier Francois, criticized more traditional auto advertising by telling Ad Age that "America had a story to tell that was bigger than any cup holder, bigger than any Columbus Day sales event."

Others called the ad a classic. "The ad broke the Internet," one ad industry blogger wrote in 2016. "Millions ran to Twitter and YouTube to re-watch the ad, and Chrysler's supplemental videos help capture eyes and hearts. Chrysler got a huge spike in online traffic and YouTube video views. (Of) consumers, surveyed just one week after the ad launched, 87% had a favorable opinion of the Chrysler brand."

Yet just five years after the most expensive ad in history debuted on a Super Bowl broadcast, the Chrysler 200 was dead, killed by budget cuts. And Chrysler was once again struggling financially, reconfiguring its lineup.

What happened? Could the critically acclaimed ad campaign, which apparently stirred sales as well as emotions for a short period of time, have anything to do with this course of events? As many asked: What did Chrysler buy for $10 million?

The headline on a story by Joann Muller, longtime Detroit bureau chief for Forbes put it this way in 2012: "Do Chrysler's TV Sermons Really Sell Any Cars?"

The answer is the subject of this book. Yes, great stories can sell products and services. They can move hearts and minds and they inspire action.

In the case of the 2011 Eminem ad for Chrysler, the story was great but it was the wrong story. And maybe the wrong story-teller. And also, did Chrysler even know what the audience really wanted to see, hear or experience in a story about the car company?

Don't misunderstand me, or the purpose of this book. The Born of Fire ad is a great piece of art. Eminem is still a top music maker, still releasing chart-topping hits a decade after the ad debuted.

The problem with the most expensive example of classic advertising ever is *not* that it's telling a bad story. It's that it's sharing the wrong story at the wrong time with the wrong audience.

The ad is not really about Chrysler at all; it's about Detroit. And as much as Detroit and Detroiters deserve a Super Bowl salute— for ingenuity, resilience and many other attributes, a successful Super Bowl ad should help Chrysler sell more cars. And while it aroused interest for a short period of time, Chrysler is still in shaky financial straits and the car at the heart of the commercial is dead.

For certain, you can't place all the blame for this on the advertising, whether it's the agency or the creatives involved or Chrysler. You *can* argue that all of these talented folks could have earned a better result if they had focused on sharing a more fundamental story, the company's Capital S Story—the story that answers the question: Why should someone buy from you, or work for you, or invest in you or partner with you?

That's the purpose of this book: To help you uncover your Capital S Story, identify the storytellers who are best equipped to share it, and provide you a framework based upon classic story archetypes that will help you earn storytelling success.

Why the Capital S Story? Because I believe you shouldn't spend *a single dollar* on your marketing unless you can tell whether that dollar is doing anything for you. And it's especially true if you're sharing the best marketing asset you have, your great untold story.

Here's what you can expect in the chapters ahead:

- Guidance on how to uncover your authentic story, and tools to help you develop the most important aspects of your authentic story;
- A process to identify the fluent storytellers in your organization who know your story best and an outline of how to develop your best storytellers to deliver success;
- A comprehensive introduction to the ageless cultural storylines and archetypes that, appropriately adapted to your company, will deliver storytelling success;

- In each chapter, a StoryCrafter's Toolkit, with links to online resources, research and tools that can help you and your organization take what you learn in this book and apply it immediately to your own storytelling.

In our first chapter, we'll begin to look at the evidence that sharing the right story is not only art, it's science. Our brains are hardwired for storytelling and science proves it. Storytelling is not some sugary frosting that you heap on whatever you sell or do; it's the essence of connecting with those you most want to reach, especially your best-fit clients. We'll also see how well-known brands effectively employ storytelling for success.

In our second chapter, we'll look at a specific experiment that validates the power of storytelling through human biology. We'll also outline how the brain uses storytelling to make sense of the world, meet more brands who do it well, and learn about the pioneers who laid the groundwork for effective storytelling—even in our time-compressed, information-overloaded 21st-century culture.

In our third chapter, we'll explore why classic advertising has become the most inauthentic purveyor of stories. We'll look at why the critical importance of sharing the right story at the right time with the right audience has been buried under a raft of irrelevant considerations. We'll learn from two of the greats who essentially invented advertising more than 100 years ago, and how their commitment to storytelling has disappeared. And we'll look at how powerful storytelling can make even the most mundane objects worthy of interest.

In chapter 4, we'll explore what it means to uncover your Capital S Story. We'll look at some of the most powerful examples of authentic storytelling and explore how a truly authentic story, shared by a fluent storyteller and continually adjusted to keep the audience engaged, drives the best results. Along the way, I'll explain how I came to be passionate about storytelling and how I earned my storytelling bona fides.

In our fifth chapter, we'll explore the experiences that led me to focus on storytelling for companies as a career and passion. We'll dig into the story of my own company to explore the application of the principles that drive your Capital S Story. And we'll meet the dozen or so most common heroes that can likely be found in every organization.

In our sixth chapter, we'll open the hood and examine the journeys of two companies in uncovering, developing and sharing their great, untold Capital S Stories. We'll explore examples of our StoryCrafting process to help bring storytelling principles to life for you as you seek your own best-fit clients through sharing your organization's Capital S Story.

In chapter 7, we'll look at the differences (and similarities) in sharing your Capital S Story if you are selling to consumers or to other businesses. We'll review great examples of business to consumer storytelling and business to business storytelling as we identify common themes and a few differences.

Social media is constantly changing—and also certain to be with us for a long time. In chapter 8, we look at how storytelling, a practice that began around a communal campfire, is just as relevant when the campfire flickers on a digital social media channel. And we'll look at what the future might hold if computers learn to share stories.

In every discipline, at some point, "professionals" with ulterior motives begin to invade the field. In chapter 9, we look at the types of inauthentic "experts" you might meet on your storytelling journey, how to identify them and how to stay true to your Capital S Story while dealing with them.

In chapter 10, our last chapter, we learn about one of the greatest examples of corporate storytelling from one of the world's best-known and most authentic brands. With a firm understanding of how to uncover and develop your organization's Capital S Story, you're now ready to go out and share that story with everyone who needs to see, hear and experience it.

There are many reasons that this book is worthy of your time.

If you are a business leader who's tired of classic advertising that doesn't deliver results, this book is for you.

If you're tired of being told that you must lie to your customers and prospects to sell to them, this book is for you.

If you don't feel your marketing captures the essence of your organization and what problems it solves for your customers, this book is for you.

If you've never understood how to make marketing work for you and you're frustrated that potential customers don't understand what you have to offer, this book is for you.

The magic button is in your pocket. Are you ready to give it a push? Let's get started!

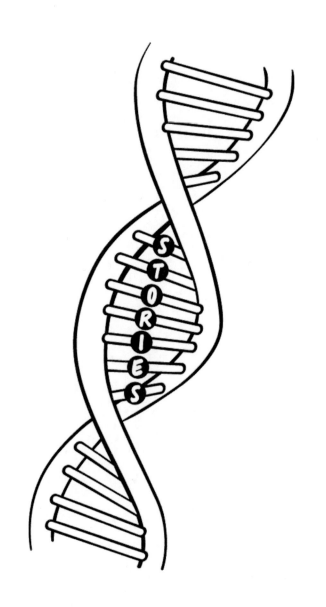

1

WHAT'S BIOLOGY GOT TO DO WITH MARKETING? STORYTELLING ISN'T BULL CRAP, IT'S BIOLOGY

Picture this: It's a fine Sunday afternoon in the crispness of late fall. Your nose tingles at the woodsy tang of your next-door neighbor's outdoor fire pit. You and yours are in the family room for your favorite team's first big rivalry game of the season. The gang is gathered around that 62-inch flat screen you're so glad you bought. The fireplace is hot and crackling, the fresh guacamole and chips are leaving just the right zing on your tongue, and the brews are going down icy cold with every sip, just the way you like them.

Then she appears, on that big screen. Her long, reddish-brown hair falls playfully over creamy cheekbones and down to her white football jersey. She's sort of half-laying, half-sitting on a big bed, playfully tossing a football while smiling into the camera. Then she speaks: "Watching football together is great. But I think women would agree, huddling with their man afterwards is nice too." Suddenly, there's more of a zing in your throat and it ain't the guac. You gaze around the room at your family, friends and your teenagers. A mixture of embarrassment and shame washes over you. You've not only been subjected to unpleasantness. You know it's a lie—the universe of women 20 years younger than men who might purchase Viagra for a little "huddling" is remarkably small.

Picture this: the following day, you're navigating the morning hustle with a gleam and a smile. The gleam comes from spending time with those closest to you yesterday, and the smile comes from the sunshine above. You feel the energy of the morning and contemplate the promise of a new week in which you lead your team to collaborate for success. Five minutes later, as the elevator pulls you toward your office, your smartphone is vibrating AND beeping. It can't be. Since the last stoplight, 14 emails already? And two calls. The doors open and you hear it before you see it: The gaggle of three waiting for you. There goes your plan. Your immediate reaction: Hit the down button and head for your car. A few minutes ago, a clear goal and sharp focus seemed so tangible you could taste it. Now you're overwhelmed by the noise of real life. You wonder how you can manage the chaos to move your team forward in the right direction.

Picture this: It's Friday night. The theater is dark and the murmur of anticipation transforms the crowd's conversation to background music before a huge, dark screen. As light fills the screen, a sea of heads spreads out before you. In your hands, the box of popcorn is hot and the buttery scent is compelling. On screen, a young woman wanders down a dark hallway, led by armed men. From the Dolby sound system, ominous piano music rains down as an interrogator recites a list of her crimes: armed insurgency, forgery of documents, and stealing, as scenes of mayhem play out. You lean forward in your seat. Off screen, an older woman's voice intones: "On your own from the age of 15—reckless, aggressive and undisciplined." The young woman responds: "This is a rebellion, isn't it? I rebel!" What are you thinking?

Three different days, three different scenarios. The same you. Which of these experiences engages you most? Which of them delivers a message you would notice and retain? And which of these will move you to think, act or feel differently once you were exposed to it?

What does each of our scenarios tell us about the answer to our question? And what does each reveal about effective (and ineffective) business communication?

While we watched our football game, we experienced one of the most enduring and classic iterations of marketing: The TV commercial. The one I picked for our little story is real and in the last few years has sold sexual enhancement medication for men during the regular NFL season and post-season. It was even parodied to hilarious effect by actor Ben Stiller on late-night TV (Stiller's version was a mirror image, with him as a man selling a product to women).

Classic advertising provokes a number of responses in us that this commercial illustrates. First, we expect advertising to lie to us. In ads selling sexual enhancement medication to men, the women making the pitch are invariably too young and too beautiful to realistically make the case. Frequently, to gain attention, advertising shares the lie by evoking a setting that grabs our attention, in this case an intentional sexual subtext (do we really want our kids watching the big game with us to see these kinds of ads?). Ultimately, while some of it is fun or humorous, classic advertising makes us defensive and puts us on guard.

Is it any surprise then, that over the last several years, the generation most important to the future of the organizations we lead—Millennials—has registered the lowest level of engagement, trust and support ever measured for classic advertising?

Our second story scenario reliably describes the world in which most of us live as business leaders. The 21st century bombards us with information, instantaneously delivered from hundreds of electronic sources from signboards to our cars to our smartphones. The immediate availability of information compels us to ignore or delete most of the messages we receive because we can't consume them in a way that helps make sense of their meaning. We figure 90 percent of those messages are garbage, and we hope we can wade through the trash well enough to retain the 10 percent of messages we expect to be legitimate.

Let's consider our third story scenario. Our example is drawn from a real movie trailer for one of the recent chapters in the *Star Wars* saga. *Star Wars* is one of the most enduring movie franchises because it is a reliable, immersive experience in powerful storytelling. When we watch a movie with a good storyline, we are literally drawn in. We relax and we participate. We're receptive because we're engaged. We suspend disbelief and are willing to place ourselves, as the opening crawl for every one of the *Star Wars* movies puts it, "A long time ago in a galaxy far, far away ..."

Don't take my word for it—consider box office sales. The Numbers, a top film industry blog, says the box office for the first eight *Star Wars* films totals more than $6.6 billion or $828 million a film. Don't like *Star Wars*? What about Harry Potter? Or James Bond? Or Lord of the Rings? What about Marvel comic heroes? These film franchises are the top five highest grossing of all time. And all, as a group, are distinguished by powerful storytelling.

Don't like movies? What about bedtime stories? Every one of us who's ever heard the "Once upon a time" mantra as the opening of our favorite childhood story—or recited it 200 nights in a row as a parent—can attest to the immersive power of stories. E.B. White's *Charlotte's Web*, first published in 1952, has entertained generations and sold more than 45 million copies in 23 languages. It's also been adapted into two movies, a stage play, and yes, a video game.

What's going on here? Quite simply, a biological imperative. We don't develop a love for story. We are *born with it*, thanks to biology. This is true of us individually and as a society. It's been true of societies since the beginning of time. Sharing your story to effectively promote your brand isn't a fad, trend or gimmick—it's biology. In fact, sharing your organization's story drives your brand and the other investments you've made in marketing.

Magnetic resonance imaging (MRI) and other brain scanning techniques, when combined with modern neuroscience, demonstrate definitively why stories work in communications.

Let's examine one example: In this Princeton University work chronicled a few years ago by Wired magazine, study researchers Greg Stephens and Uri Hasson discovered that effective storytelling literally creates something that the good Vulcan Mr. Spock could only fake in the Star Trek movies and on TV: a mind meld between the storyteller and the audience.

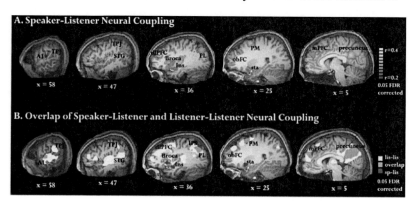

What do we see in the images above? Over the course of time, as an effective storyteller shares a story, good storytelling literally causes changes in the brain activity of the audience receiving the storyteller's message. It becomes like a great dance team—like Fred Astaire and Ginger Rogers. First, the storyteller and audience begin (x-58), then the storyteller leads (x-47, x-36) and the audience ultimately responds and connects (x-25). Across this series of images, you can see how this plays out, the storyteller and audience playing off each other, sometimes coming together, sometimes moving in response to the other.

This technology gives us a picture inside the brain of what most of us have experienced repeatedly in our lives but which we couldn't previously quantify: the speaker who had us in the palm of his hand, the movie that left us with profound images and thoughts days after we saw it; the concert that kept coming back to us in song, sound and picture a week after we attended it. How often have you (or someone you know), said something to the effect of "I wish that concert/movie/play never ended, I was so caught up in it and enjoyed it so much." That's what we're seeing in the series of pictures above.

This is the science that matches the powerful cultural history that advocates for storytelling in business. As humans, we've been sharing stories since before we had written language. There's been a historical, compelling anecdotal sense that we keep doing that for a reason—because it works. Thanks to MRIs and other tools that allow us to see our brains at work, we now have the scientific evidence to measure the anecdotal and prove the power of storytelling.

Findings like these have profound impact for the way business leaders need to be thinking about the power of storytelling in business. Business storytelling is no longer a matter of costumes and characters and entertainment in terms of how information is presented.

Business storytelling is now a powerful tool that's scientifically, demonstrably effective in communicating with the audiences that you most need to reach. In fact, the most important communications asset your organization owns is its story.

Storytelling has the power to engage the audiences you need to reach and deliver a message at the deepest human level, the power to create a memory. Story's power to create a memory comes from the ingrained power of our shared human experience. Great storytellers, including George Lucas, the man behind the *Star Wars* franchise, tap classic storylines and character roles—known as archetypes—that are easily under-stood even in our information-saturated 21st-century environ-ment because they have played out over and over in human history. They carry names and roles ranging from ruler to explorer to outlaw to everyman.

Think of Robin Hood, or Dirty Harry. Their archetype is The Outlaw. Luke Skywalker in *Star Wars* is also a classic outlaw character. Each of these antihero/hero characters experience a storyline we will explore later in the book known as *the hero's journey*. It's not the only storyline that's relevant for us as business leaders—we will explore others later—but the hero's journey is an example of a storyline that packs an engaging and memorable punch. The importance of archetypes is the power they give us to share our story in ways that are unique, compel-ling and memorable.

Are you taking advantage of your story in your marketing efforts? How are you promoting your brand today? What's the ratio of money and attention you are devoting to classic adver-tising and lies, or colors and logos, as opposed to the powerful narrative that explains why your organization is the right choice for customers, employees, investors or strategic partners? Is it possible that you're missing out on a powerhouse at your fingertips—your story?

You don't have to be a great brand to unlock the power of storytelling. But let's start by looking at a few of the world's great brands of the last few decades and consider how we embrace their stories. Your own business may not be world famous, but we can learn and apply a great deal from the stories of those that are.

Nike is famous for athletic apparel that makes it possible for the weekend warrior to feel he or she is on a par with Tiger Woods or Michael Jordan. The swoosh logo and the "Just Do It" mantra are easily remembered "brand assets," and so are the relationships with star athletes including Jordan, Woods and others.

Those relationships and brand assets *represent* the Nike story—they are not the story. The story itself runs much deeper. The Nike story gives life and meaning to those relationships and those brand assets.

The real Nike story is Bill Bowerman, the legendary University of Oregon track coach who ruined his wife's waffle iron trying to make a sole for a better running shoe for his athletes. Even though Bowerman was great enough to coach 31 Olympic athletes, 51 All-Americans, 12 American record-holders, 22 NCAA champions and 16 sub-4 minute milers, he couldn't find a suitable running shoe for his athletes until he made one himself. And he couldn't make that shoe a success until one of his former athletes, miler Phil Knight, helped him found the company we know today as Nike.

Today everything Nike does, from endorsements to slogans, is an outward reflection of the Nike story. It's the power of the story that propels Nike forward, not its colors, logos or slogans. We may not see the relationship between the Nike story and its brand until someone points it out to us. Nike sees it. That's why the company's employee Number Four, Nelson Farris, carries the title of chief storyteller.

To revisit our discussion about archetypes a bit earlier, Nike represents a champion archetype—not in the sense of being the winning athlete itself, but in the sense of *being the champion that makes your individual success possible*, whether you are an Olympic athlete or a weekend runner.

Nike is hardly the only example of a well-known company that understands a great brand is a natural outgrowth of its story. Since its founding, Southwest Airlines has played the part of the underdog—another outlaw archetype example—in the airline industry. Southwest's success today makes the company the most-valued airline in the world and one of the world's most valued public companies.

The Southwest story didn't start that way, and the company has never forgotten that beginning. Even before its first flight, Southwest's story has been about affordable air travel. In the beginning, co-founders Rollin King and Herb Kelleher wanted to make it as affordable to fly from city to city as it was to take the bus. At the beginning, competitors who'd grown rich and comfortable on federally regulated air travel saw the upstart Southwest as a threat, and they conspired to kill it, in court, in private arm-twisting with Southwest's bankers, and even in the U.S. Congress.

At every turn, as its much more powerful competitors tried to kill it, Southwest embraced the adversity it faced and made it part of the Southwest story. Just a few examples:

To deprive Southwest of traffic, competitors got regulators to force Southwest to fly out of old Love Field in Dallas, which at the time had just been replaced by what we know today as Dallas/Fort Worth International, a brand-new airport. Competitors hoped the move would kill Southwest. Instead, Southwest embraced Love Field and made it its own. In its early years, flying Southwest meant munching on Love Nuts instead of peanuts, and sipping Love Potions instead of cocktails. When Southwest's success made it a public company, Kelleher and his team knew the three-letter stock symbol they wanted: LUV, for Love Field.

Another example: Most fliers know Southwest maintains one of the best on-time records in the industry, but few know why. It's one of the most important aspects of the Southwest story and brand.

Even before Southwest had flown its first flight, its competitors had gotten to its bankers and convinced them to tighten the purse strings. Southwest, still several weeks from its first flight, had been lucky enough to lease four Boeing 737s for its fleet.

As its bankers bowed to Southwest's competitors and turned the screws, Kelleher and his team were faced with a terrible choice: Lay off a sizable percentage of its staff, even before its first flight, or give up a plane. Southwest called an all-employee meeting and took a vote. The result: get rid of a plane and commit to somehow figuring out how to make as many flights with three planes as Southwest had planned to make with four. This change pushed the Southwest team to innovate "turnaround" procedures that still lead the industry. They are also a core aspect of the company's story and culture. The same discipline Southwest applied to that adversity has become part of how the company has approached challenge after challenge.

So when we see TV ads that proclaim, "you are now free to move about the country," or see Southwest employees in airports "freeing" passengers from the tyrannical behaviors of other airlines, we are indeed seeing clever marketing and a memorable brand. There is no lying involved! We are experiencing the brand as something much more than cute. We see and hear the brand as we do because it is a direct representation of the company's story, as with Nike.

You don't need to be a big, recognizable brand for storytelling to work. Consider Blendtec, a 40-year-old company in Orem, Utah that just happens to make some of the most durable commercial and home blenders in the world.

Like far too many companies, Blendtec and its founder Tom Dickson toiled in relative obscurity for decades, growing nicely while focusing primarily on making indestructible, powerful machines. Everybody at Blendtec knew those powerful machines were the essence of the company story, the reason customers bought and relied on Blendtec. Yet that story wasn't part of the company's marketing until George Wright joined the company. In 2006, while walking down the hall one day, Wright happened to see Dickson, a folksy gray-haired kids' vision of a mad scientist, wearing a white coat and tossing an object into a Blendtec blender to test it. Inspiration struck. Wright learned that Dickson tested the blenders by grinding unusual objects in them to prove their seemingly limitless power, thereby wowing skeptical potential clients. Wright saw that Blendtec had a story. And now they had a marketer who seized the story.

Within weeks, Wright and Dickson had collaborated to produce the first *Will it Blend?* video for the relatively new social media channel called YouTube. Dickson's videos, in which he's blended everything from rotisserie chickens and Coca-Cola to different models of iPhones, drove sales. Since 2007, *Will It Blend?* videos have been viewed 265 million times on YouTube and helped produce millions in sales. Dickson has become an international celebrity. He's demonstrated Blendtec blenders on NBC's *Today* and for many other media outlets. The cheeky comedic genius of how Blendtec markets its products has put the company in the spotlight time and again.

While often corny and sometimes gimmicky, the Blendtec *Will It Blend?* effort works because it is a natural (if quirky) out-growth of an essential tenet of the company's story. Dickson represents yet another of our classic—and successful—story archetypes, the jester. He makes us laugh—and helps us to buy.

Compare the Blendtec approach to that of our TV commercial at the beginning of this chapter. Tom Dickson is nowhere near lying when he's selling blenders. Can there be anything more authentic (and fun) than using your product to bring to life every four-year-old's dream of smashing practically anything you want and getting paid to do it? It's magic.

If someone could give you a magic button that unlocked the essential power of your company's story so *you* could convince people to buy, would you push it? What if I told you that you already have that button? It's been in your proverbial pocket for some time. Since most of us view marketing as some variation on classic advertising or "interruption marketing" techniques, we've never bothered to push it.

It's time that we do. As our examples illustrate, some of the world's most successful companies have been pushing the story button and winning for quite some time. Every organization has a magic button that can unlock the power of its story. Nike's power comes from being a champion. Southwest's power comes from being an outlaw. Blendtec's power comes from a willingness to play the jester.

Where does your company story draw its power? You might not think your story is that powerful—but it is. If you don't know if your story is that powerful, it's time to uncover it.

These companies understand that the power of their story attracts and engages their best-fit clients. As our Blendtec example illustrates, you don't have to be a mega company or have a dramatic history to deliver results. You just have to understand the power of your authentic story.

So what exactly *does it mean* to be authentic when storytelling?

First and foremost, your story must be rooted in fact and transparently genuine. In film or literature, great works pull us in so deeply that we suspend disbelief about the ability to fly, travel through time and many other seemingly impossible situations that, in real life, would be entirely inauthentic.

As business leaders, we work in real life, so we must use the powerful tools of fictional storytelling with great care. This is especially true in our 21st-century, social media-driven culture.

Inauthenticity earns swift and painful rebuke in our wired world.

So how does this work in real life? If you and I witness an auto accident from opposite corners of the same intersection, it's likely we see different aspects of the event. When a police officer interviews us about the accident, and we share different versions, does that mean one of us is telling the truth and one of us is lying? No. Our recollections, based upon the same set of facts, are equally authentic. They are just different.

This is a critical distinction lost on far too many business leaders who want to share their story. In nearly any situation in life, there is more than one version of the same story. And that's OK, as long as it's rooted in fact and genuine, meaning that while it may be structured to persuade an audience, it's easy to trace that persuasion to an interpretation of facts that's genuine.

Our hearts and minds are always searching for authenticity, the interpretation of facts that gives us a clear picture, the language that rings right, the experience that makes us feel comfortable. This is why the scene in which Dorothy's dog Toto pulls back the curtain in the 1939 film, *The Wizard of Oz,* is so well remembered—it illustrates this timeless human principle of authenticity. In the film, the larger-than-life, loud and frightening Wizard is revealed by Toto's yank at the curtain to be a fairly ordinary man using a machine to make himself something he is not.

As a former journalist and now public relations executive for the better part of the last four decades, I've been continually exposed to the full power of *authentic* story in practically every conceivable format.

I came of age journalistically in the era of Woodward and Bernstein, the two Washington Post reporters who broke the story of the Watergate break-in scandal in 1973. That scandal ended the presidency of Richard M. Nixon when their reporting and Congressional hearings revealed that the story the president and his staff told the American people about the break-in of the Watergate offices of the opposing political party was a lie—it was the president and his campaign staff who undertook the break-in, contrary to what they had claimed. Their story was a lie, and Nixon resigned in disgrace, remembered for uttering the phrase, "I am not a crook."

The Watergate fallout made the profession of journalism and its demand for authenticity, an important concept we'll define later, exceedingly popular. I proudly wore a T-shirt in those years that proclaimed: "If your mother says she loves you, check it out."

In the decades since, the public view of journalism has swung wildly. Today many news consumers may hold some level of contempt for the news media, while still consuming "news."

It's easy perhaps to focus on the messenger and miss the importance of the message. The message is what this book is all about. No form of communication better carries a message than story. And no source of stories is more vibrant in terms of the vast expanse of human experience than journalism, regardless of how you or I or your Uncle Burt might feel about journalists. We'll talk in later chapters about the emergence of "user-generated content" that often competes with news content. And we'll touch on the true meaning of authenticity.

In recent years, the emergence of what has been branded "fake news" has added another layer of confusion to understanding the importance of authenticity and stories rooted in fact. This is a book about the human experience, so by its very nature we will deal with definitions of truth and a lack of truth appropriately. This is not a political book, nor is it a polemic or commentary on the division and distrust that we see in today's popular culture and civic society. It's not my intent to engage in that debate. There are other authors with far more experience (and many with far more charged opinions) who can dissect the trajectory of our political discourse and provide levels of insight specific to that debate.

The relevance of journalistic storytelling for our purposes is two-fold: It's our richest vein of stories relating the human experience. I've been immersed in that world for the better part of four decades. This gives me a particularly deep well of personal experience to draw on as we explore the kinds of stories that connect best with the audiences we must reach to drive success in our organizations.

All the foment about "fake news" makes authentic storytelling–and your story–more important than ever. The cynicism and skepticism that's permeated the brains of any audience you hope to reach now demands proof of authenticity and a commitment to truth telling. In this regard, the core subject of this book has never been more important. We are already bombarded by too much information, coming at us too quickly. Political division has created another critical imperative to share your authentic story.

In the 21st century, public opinion polls show that a majority of Americans expect politicians to lie. This is not just our political reality—it's the reality we face in business as well.

If anything, the world of marketing is worse. Some of the best in the business playfully and disingenuously write books with titles such as *All Marketers Are Liars*. Is it any wonder that the same polls that place politicians, government and journalists in low regard find more than half of the public distrustful of classic advertising?

Far too many marketers busily wrap liars and lies in new skins to worm their way into our minds and pocketbooks. This is exactly what our world doesn't need. It is in direct conflict with the needs of our information-soaked, always-on 21st-century world. Transparency is the new buzzword to describe the concept that if you lie, we will all be on the internet in five minutes to find out you're lying now, that you lied before and that your momma always thought you were gonna be a liar.

I became a public relations and marketing practitioner in part because journalism taught me that some of the best stories of people and organizations in this world will not be shared unless someone makes the effort to understand the authentic storyline at the heart of every great organization.

What does a successful company story look like? The most successful stories are what I call Capital S Stories. There is a profound difference between a Capital S Story and all others.

In the old days, when people actually read newspapers in hard copy, *small s* stories were those read one day, then fed into the bottom of the birdcage the next. In today's world, the *small s* stories are those that fly by on social media, the ones you can't remember 10 minutes later.

Your Capital S Story answers the most central question of your company's existence: Why should someone buy from you, work for you, invest in you or partner with you. Your Capital S Story answers fundamental questions about these relationships that go far beyond features and benefits. They speak to the very character and commitment of the organization and its people. Capital S Stories are the ones with staying power. They continue to command attention over time. They are at the heart of our journey ahead. And what does that journey hold in store for you?

We've been sharing stories as human beings since before we had written language. Now you have the opportunity to turn biology, culture and science to your benefit, engaging your best-fit clients.

As you'll see in the pages to come, business storytelling is a powerful tool that's scientifically, demonstrably effective in communicating with the audiences you most need to reach.

StoryCrafter's Toolkit
Chapter 1

If you're reading the printed edition of the book, access these links and resources through your web browser at: capitalsstory.com/storycrafterstoolkit.

If you're reading an electronic edition, just click the links in this box to access all the resources.

- The 25 most popular bedtime stories of all time
- Wired Magazine article on Princeton University research
- Goodnight Moon back story, from Wikipedia.org
- History of the Nike 'Just Do It' campaign
- Top-performing movie franchises, ranked
- From Forbes: Millennials don't respond to ads
- OneSpot: The science of storytelling infographic

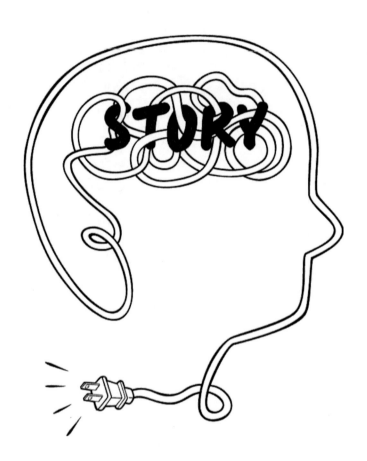

2

OUR BRAINS:
HARDWIRED FOR STORY,
HUNGRY FOR MEANING

Inside the long, dark tube, two alternating magnets encircle a young woman, bombarding her with a strength 50,000 times that of Earth's magnetic fields, mapping her every brainwave. Meanwhile, a specially designed microphone records her every thought. In a nearby control room, scientists stare at the young woman's brainwaves on a monitor and hang on every word of her story.

The young woman's voice comes from deep inside the long, dark, metal cylinder, faint, somewhat girlish, with a hint of shy humor:

"I was a freshman in high school in Miami, Florida ... and this boy Charles asks me out. He's British, he's a junior, and he's really cute but sort of shy ... So I say yes, I'm excited. He comes and picks me up in this really old, beat-up white Toyota, and he has two tapes in his car: Queen and Oasis. And so I ask him if he only listens to English bands when I get in the car and he gets a little offended. So I knew that, um, it just wasn't gonna work out with us."

The young woman's first audience is the group of scientists, led by Dr. Uri Hasson of Princeton University. Over the course of several weeks, they will share the girl's story again and again, ultimately sliding 30 young people in the long, dark cylinder, recording their every reaction to an audio recording of the young woman's story. The goal is to study the neurological reactions of the 30 individuals, none of whom know this girl or her story.

"And then we actually go out again and it's also awkward," the young woman says. *"And then the next day at school ... we're sort of with other people talking about prom, which is now months and months away ... But for some reason, out of the blue, he asks me to go to his prom with him. And, I mean, I'm a freshman girl, and it's really exciting, I never would have thought of going to the prom as a freshman, so of course I say yes, not really thinking about it."*

Each of the 30 people who slide inside the long tube, called a functional Magnetic Resonance Imaging machine, or fMRI for short, draw the same attention from the scientists as the young woman herself did. The scientists eagerly monitor their brainwaves and vital statistics, as deep inside the dark, they listen to the young woman's story for the first time:

"And then that weekend I was at a party on the beach at this big house that was like the party house of my high school ... and I'm getting a beer out of the keg and I had never really done that much so of course I'm horrible at it and it's like 85% foam, and I notice that the guy behind me is this guy Amir. He's this really good-looking senior and well, my high school was a really big swimming high school. A lot of people went there for swimming from all over the world, and so it was half a boarding school also, so there was a boys' dorm and a girls' dorm."

As Dr. Hasson and his colleagues observe their 30 subjects inside the fMRI, they begin to notice startling patterns in the brainwaves of listeners: *Their brainwave activity mirrors the activity of the young woman's brain, as she records her story.*

Dr. Hasson's study is one of many to demonstrate that storytelling is not an experience in which the storyteller is fully engaged and the audience is passive. Science demonstrates that authentic storytelling is an immersive experience for both parties, as effective in moving the hearts and minds of the audience as it is in giving the storyteller some cardiovascular exercise.

"Amir was a swimmer and he lived in the boys' dorm. And he was sort of a popular senior guy. And so he takes over and pours me this beer, of course perfectly foamless. And as he's passing it back to me, the guy behind me gets pushed or something, and pushes into me, and of course I spill the beer all over Amir, and that's how we meet. And it's sort of this high school romance fantasy, where we were just totally smitten. And so we start going out, and it's really fun. I don't have my license at this point, I have a permit, and so he teaches me how to drive. He lives in the boys' dorm and so his friends and him put me in a box, a cardboard box, and wrapped it up, and actually carried me, snuck me into the dorm as like a package. It was very funny, it was all fun, I was very happy. And then so we've been together for over two months or so and it comes time for people to kind of start talking about prom."

What's most amazing about this is what's happening inside the brains of the 30-some participants in the experiment. The fMRI is simply a high-tech variation of a camera capturing a moment. The fMRI isn't causing the interactions between the storyteller and her audience—the source is something biological in the brains of the storyteller and 30 listeners. Despite being stuffed inside the hostile environment of a banging, clanging hospital fMRI machine, the storyteller and audience somehow move in harmony 30 different times. It's remarkable.

"So at this point I've basically forgotten that Charles was even there and just assumed that we both realized that it wasn't really working out and went our separate ways. And he knew that I was now with Amir and I just assumed it was fine. But so I'm at school and I'm sitting in the quad and Charles comes

over to me and he sits down and says, 'I just wanted to you know discuss with you our plans for prom'. And I'm like 'um, I, um ...' I just didn't know what to say. So, I feel really badly about it, he obviously was, uh, hurt, and not going to let it go. And I felt badly, so I decide that I'm going to go to the prom with Charles and just meet up with Amir after."

To test their findings, Dr. Hasson and his colleagues repeat the experiment, this time with a foreign language speaker. The results aren't the same. Dr. Hasson and his colleagues know their test subjects don't understand the foreign language. They are looking for some way to eliminate the possibility that the storytelling itself could be responsible for the harmonious union of brains between storyteller and audience that their research is uncovering. The control fails—as the scientists watch their monitors, again and again, nothing happens as the storyteller speaks in a foreign language (Russian). Yet when the story is shared in English, some biological imperative unfolds on their screens: first the brainwaves of the storyteller, pulsing and lighting up certain sectors of her brain. Then, each listener's brain, its patterns at first disconnected from those of the storyteller. As the story proceeds, each listener's brain is drawn deeper and deeper into the narrative. The scientists watch this in real time.

"So then the day of the prom comes around, and on top of all of this sort of drama with this boy situation, my family ... We all decide to get certified for scuba diving. And of course ... the only weekends we can do it are the weekend before the prom and the weekend of the prom. So ... we left at like 8 in the morning, we're supposed to get back at 3. So I think ok, this is fine, I'll get back home by like 4 and I'll have like two hours to get ready for this prom. Which is a really big deal, especially as a freshman girl, I was really nervous about prom in general."

While most of the listeners in the experiment may have attended their high school prom, they certainly didn't have the same experience as the young woman sharing her story. So why are their brains reacting as if they were right alongside the young storyteller on her crazy prom date?

"So anyway, we're getting back, we've scuba dived ... and of course the boat breaks down. So ... we finally get back, and we're pulling into my house at like 6 o'clock, like two and a half hours late, just as Charles, who's always on time, of course, is pulling up ... And, I don't know if you've ever been scuba diving, but pretty much the worst you'll ever look is after you go scuba diving. You've been under 60 feet of water, which is two atmospheres of pressure, for an hour and a half. You have a goggle mark permanently sketched into your face, which takes like 5 hours to get rid of that. And um, just your hair, it's just a mess, you're just a mess. And now I have approximately 5 minutes to get ready for the prom. So I'm like trying to put on make-up while my sister is shaving my legs, while my mom is brushing my hair. And I sort of put it all together as quickly as possible, throw on a dress, and leave ... We finally get to the prom and I'm looking around for Amir, and I can't find him anywhere. So I go to the bathroom, and I come back and I hear shouting in the back corner."

Based on the biological brain changes they see on their monitors, the scientists come to a clear conclusion: storytelling moves hearts and minds. The storyteller is pulling her audience along at an unconscious level because of their shared experience of the story, of a scenario they recognize as a prom story. In a 2010 paper Dr. Hasson and his colleagues publish on this study, *Speaker–Listener Neural Coupling Underlies Successful Communication*, the scientists put it this way: "coupling (between storyteller and audience) emerges only while engaged in shared communication."

"And Amir is just totally drunk and is starting a fight with Charles. He's like about to hit him. And I run over and I grab Amir and we leave ... We decide to go to the after party pretty much immediately ... And Amir is going through his pockets to find his keys ... and he trips in the parking lot over one of those parking space indicator things ... so he just falls flat on his face. And he looks up and there's blood running out of his nose and all over and he's just a bloody mess. So I run back to the bathroom and I get paper towels and whatnot and I clean him up a bit."

Dr. Hasson and the team not only find harmony between storyteller and audience as the audience follows the story. They also find that when the audience is in sync with the storyteller, listeners' brainwaves actually *anticipate* the next step in the story. Here's how they put it:

> "The anticipatory responses may provide the listeners with more time to process an input and can compensate for problems with noisy or ambiguous input ... comprehension is facilitated by highly predictable upcoming words. Remarkably, the extent of the listener's anticipatory brain responses was highly correlated with the level of understanding, indicating that successful communication requires the active engagement of the listener."

"And we get in the car and just start driving and I'm thinking this has been the most absurd day, but of course I thought that way too soon because we're driving and Amir is like playing air guitar or something in the passenger seat and ... there was a car accident in one of these turning lanes. And I'm driving slowly, there's lights and traffic and stuff so I'm not going quickly at all ... And Amir, I'm not exactly sure what he does, but he sort of grabs my arm and I sort of turn, and I end up crashing into this accident that's already there ... it was a very light hit, no cars were ruined or anything, but the police are already there, and all of the people are already there, like

they're all watching it happen. So the policeman comes over, and I don't have my license, by the way. I have a permit so I can be driving with Amir cause he's 18, but he's wasted, I mean, he's still playing air guitar when the policeman comes over and his face is bloody. And so I give him my permit and the registration and he's like uh I need his license, so I give him Amir's license as well. And I'm thinking I'm done for. I'm thinking I'm going to jail for driving without a license with this drunk dude and I'm thinking it's all over for me."

One way to understand the interaction between storyteller and audience in this story is to think of dancing—a couple together on the floor, one leading and one following, perfectly in sync and moving through a full sensory experience, caught up in the moment. There's truth to that old quote that famed 1930s film star and dancer Ginger Rogers did everything her partner Fred Astaire did—just backwards in high heels.

Think about it for a moment: Doing something backwards and at a physical disadvantage seems illogical. Yet science proves that this is how our brains work when caught up in a great story. We aren't inside the storyteller's head; we didn't experience whatever story the storyteller is sharing firsthand. Yet we are willing to suspend disbelief, to be immersed in a joint emotional experience with the storyteller.

"So the policeman leaves and I'm really freaking out. And he comes back like 20 minutes later, and, I'm not lying, he hands me back my license and he says to me, 'I'm sorry ... but somehow your registration has blown away and I cannot find it'. And he was so embarrassed about losing my registration that he tells me to drive on my way. For real. So I drive away as quickly as I can and I finally get to the after party house and I get out of the car and Amir passes out on the beach and I call my mom and have her pick me up. And that's it."

Chances are that the story in the study resonates with you—and you don't have to be inside an fMRI for that to happen. Why? It could be because you were a teenager once. It could be that you've experienced (or witnessed) a drunken moment of teenage rebellion. It could because, even if you never went to your prom, you've seen and heard enough bad prom stories (how about the 1980s film classic, *Pretty in Pink*?). Chances are that you relate to this story in some way. We've all had similar experiences. The story resonates with you even though it's a teenager sharing her story as only a teenager can. The story sparks a response. Why?

Dr. Hasson's study is one of dozens that confirm a foundational fact: Our brains are hardwired for story. Our biology craves stories, and the Princeton study demonstrates that our brains engage with stories that we recognize. So if we're sharing a good story and we've successfully engaged our audience, why is it that our audience will do more than hang on every word: Why will they anticipate it?

STORIES: THE UTMOST DÉJÀ VU ALL OVER AGAIN

Why would our listeners be anticipating our story if they've never heard it before? While it's true that our listeners may not have experienced *our version* of that story, they probably have seen or heard or experienced a similar storyline previously.

To put it another way, while we understand stories as individuals, as human beings, we also have a *collective memory* that's built into our very genes. The research of scientists in several disciplines over the last hundred years has confirmed the evidence that we share a collective memory of stories that define our existence as humans.

Some researchers believe there is a core set of ancient stories that live in what the legendary psychiatrist Carl Jung called our "collective unconscious." Jung (1875-1961) was a practicing psychoanalyst in Switzerland at the intersection of European countries as World War I erupted around him. Through his practice, Jung discovered that despite differences in language, culture or ethnicity, his patients all had the same nightmares and dreams.

In the chapters ahead, we'll explore the ancient stories and the power they possess. We'll learn how to share your authentic business story in ways that tap into the collective unconscious. For now, let's take a look at a few examples of what we'll call *archetypes*, to get your imagination started.

In the last 50 years, the collective power of classic storytelling and archetypes emerged from the work of mythologist Joseph Campbell (1904-1987), who was inspired by Jung. For Campbell, the greatest stories of all time come from the most important stories our societies have shared since the beginning of civilization—origin stories. How humans came to be, why the sun rises, whether or not some divine being or beings is responsible for our world and our existence.

While he was a young man Campbell had the good fortune to travel the world and see cultures across Asia, Africa and many places most Westerners had not seen. Along the way, he lived and worked for a time alongside the novelist John Steinbeck and even helped explore the remote Canadian Passage with the explorer Ed Ricketts (said to be the model for the character of Doc in Steinbeck's novel *Cannery Row* and others).

A scholar who taught in later years at Sarah Lawrence College, Campbell was fluent in English, Latin, Sanskrit, French, German and Japanese, which made it possible for him to experience the stories of a much wider variety of cultures in their original languages—something few storytelling scholars had accomplished before or since.

In our first chapter, I shared some of the *Star Wars* storyline to illustrate the power of storytelling as Campbell came to understand it. The central character's journey in *Star Wars* follows an ancient storyline that Campbell dubbed *The Hero's Journey*. In this storyline, the hero or heroine begins as an outcast or outlaw, meets a magician, gains some fantastical power and returns to his or her society to save the day.

George Lucas, the creator of the *Star Wars* franchise, worked closely with Campbell in developing the storyline of the original *Star Wars* films so they would follow Campbell's outline of the hero's journey. Lucas built his scripts around the classic hero archetype that Campbell described. We all know how that turned out.

In his several books, Campbell claimed that throughout human history, regardless of time, place, economic attainment or intellectual advancement, societies told and retold the same stories, most especially the hero's journey. In Western civilization, Robin Hood and Clint Eastwood's character in the Dirty Harry movies are both variations on the hero's journey.

While it's the best-known classic storyline or archetype, the hero's journey is hardly the only ancient story that lives in our collective unconscious. We'll explore many of them in the chapters to come. For now, let's look at one more to illustrate the variety and the success of tapping storylines that have their roots in our collective unconscious.

In the Bridget Jones books and films, the heroine at first represents a common story of the innocent—think Cinderella or Rapunzel—the woman waiting for the white knight to save her. We all recognize this ancient story. We've encountered it more times than we can count.

The Bridget Jones story has an immediate modern twist to the ancient story of the innocent. It's quickly clear in the plot that while a lot of Bridget's journey is about finding the right partner, it's also a journey of discovery for an underdog, a heroine ready to shake off the obstacles in her path to emerge as the woman she really is. This is the same twist we see in many of Disney's successful recent animated franchises, from *Mulan* to *Frozen*.

The transformation becomes clear in the first of Helen Fielding's three Bridget Jones books, *Bridget Jones's Diary*, when she writes (in Bridget's voice) that: "... we were always taught, instead of waiting to be swept off our feet, to 'expect little, forgive much'." Immediately after this comes out, Bridget becomes the archetypical underdog who finds her voice and her purpose and the story takes a different and very interesting turn. As Fielding puts it in the novel, "One must not live one's life through men but must be complete on oneself as a woman of substance."

Classic storylines are for business as much as they are for fantasy. Consider the story of Sheryl Sandberg, COO of Facebook, the social networking behemoth. Throughout her career, Sandberg has demonstrated a life lived as a woman of substance. In 2013, her first book, *Lean In*, became a runaway bestseller and inspired a movement of female executives to challenge the kind of societal and personal norms that feed cultural storylines of women as dependent upon men.

Sandberg's example as a female leader living a classic and powerful storyline took a significant (and tragic) step forward in 2015 when her husband Dave Goldberg died while they were on vacation with her family in Mexico. At her husband's sudden death, Sandberg told a friend she had to pursue Option B in her life, to which her friend responded, "Then kick the shit out of Option B."

This storyline—a variation on the adage that when life gives you lemons, you make lemonade—has added a new chapter to Sandberg's real-life story of empowerment. The phrase has taken on a life of its own on the internet, and by sharing it, Sandberg has inspired yet another movement powered by an easily understandable (and collective) storyline, brought to life.

From the works of Jung and Campbell, we can identify as many as 12 or 13 distinct character profiles or storylines that we tell in the 21st century. In later chapters, we'll explore many more real-life, business adaptations of classic storylines. For now, these adaptations of classic storylines, or archetypes, are introductory examples. We'll see that archetypes have endless variations. When the right archetype is matched with the right authentic story, storytelling moves hearts and minds in ways that deliver unmatched results—more effective communication with an engaged audience, which creates a measurable return on investment.

STORIES AND THE BRAIN: OLD, OLDER, OLDEST

In 2010, the search engine Google estimated that our modern society creates more information every two days than had existed in the entire world from the dawn of time to 2003. Is it any wonder then, that in today's message tsunami, we especially rely on story for meaning? After all, this biological response to incoming information has been with us since the beginning of human history.

Scientists have come to understand that the human brain, while complex, can be described as having three major functional areas that fit together.

As an advanced 21st-century global civilization, we like to spend our energy on what is known as the "neocortex," the "newest" part of our brain, which can be considered merely old. It includes those clusters of structures that help us understand abstract concepts, including planning, modeling and simulation. This is the part of our brain typically associated with rational thought.

Our older brain, sometimes called the "limbic brain," includes areas of the brain responsible for our social and nurturing behaviors. This is the part of our brain many scientists link to our desire as humans to live in families and communities, and for our desire to parent and nurture.

At the "oldest" level is what some scientists have called the "reptilian brain," because it is shared with creatures whose brains lack the capability for sophisticated reasoning. This part of our brain controls functions at the subconscious level, including breathing. In their 2015 paper, scientists Sharad Agarwal and Tanusree Dutta claim that as much as 90 percent of the information that reaches our brains is processed subconsciously.

Their research, and the research of many others, has led to the creation of a science called neuromarketing, which applies the neuroscientific working of the brain to understanding how to create successful communications.

In our oldest brain, story helps us make sense of whether we should fight or flee, of whether we should pay attention or ignore information. Christophe Morin, co-author of the 2007 book *Neuromarketing* and a principal in the company Sales-Brain, identifies six subconscious stimuli of the old brain, inputs that are:

1. **Self-Centered**: Is anything affecting your immediate survival?
2. **Contrasting**: Do you see a tiger in the tall grass ahead or is that merely a shadow?
3. **Visual**: Do you see a snake? OK, a snake can kill you! Move!
4. **Tangible**: Is this something you know, or if you don't, something that you can touch and evaluate?
5. **Emotional**: Do you see, hear or experience something that immediately stirs you to react by crying, laughing

or engaging in some other emotional response without thinking about it?

6. **Self-Contained**: Do you detect a beginning and an end? In other words, is this a story, and can you follow it? Your attention span is short and so you'll pay attention to the beginning and perk up at the end.

Why might a beginning and end be important at the level of the unthinking, survival-driven brain? Biology provides the answer. Inside your cranium or mine, the brain's mass represents just 3 percent of overall body weight. Because of what we need our brains to do, though, they consume a full 23 percent of our overall energy. So biology built our brains to be the original energy-saving appliance. When the brain determines that it doesn't need to pay attention to something, it shuts down.

This is why college freshmen sleep through the middle of boring lectures, why we ignore TV commercials and why traditional advertising fails to engage your prospects in ways that will deliver results.

All of us have experienced this personally. My own best example is from the 1988 Democratic convention in Atlanta, which I covered as a journalist. On the opening night of the convention, a young, southern governor with presidential ambitions rose to nominate the party's choice for president.

Expectations were high—this was a prime-time talk right before the late evening news across America. Unfortunately, the speaker and his speech lacked any storytelling. Across the convention hall of 10,000, and across America before millions of flickering TV screens, the reptilian brains of citizens went to sleep.

So when the speaker finally wrapped up—33 minutes later—I watched from the press box as 10,000 reptilian brains across the convention woke up as the speaker uttered the words, "In conclusion." I mean the delegates stood, they cheered, they applauded, and they clapped and whistled—because the speech was over.

Governor Bill Clinton of Arkansas could hardly have done worse that night. The *Arkansas Democrat*, the major paper in his home state, called his speech "an unmitigated disaster. A gentler, more charitable assessment would be less than honest, considering the reaction of delegates, network commentators and the national press."

Of course, Bill Clinton has his own story, and this speech was but part of one chapter. Clinton later earned a reputation as a great storyteller and speaker.

What biology demonstrates is that when a story paints the right picture for us, when it resonates with us, when we feel as if we are a character inside the narrative itself, we drop our defenses and start participating in the story. We stop resisting and begin belonging. We become energetic and interactive. Traditional advertising doesn't do this. It can't because traditional advertising isn't inviting us into a shared experience—it's selling us something we may or may not want or need at that point in time, using images and gimmickry that we may inherently distrust. Authentic stories engage us when we are ready, in ways that unlock the internal power of our brain's biology.

When we experience a film such as *Star Wars* or *Bridget Jones's Diary,* the full immersion of our senses activates the old brain. What we see, hear and *feel* while sitting in a darkened movie theater pulls our brains along for the ride—it's as if we are inside the movie. Great cinema (especially action and horror flicks) has evoked this response for decades; now we have that fMRI science to prove that, yes, we're imagining things *and we're also experiencing them as if we were there.*

Companies such as Mindsign Neuromarketing are now using fMRI to measure the effectiveness of film storytelling in engaging our brains. Mindsign employed its science for *Avatar* director James Cameron. Take a look at this YouTube clip (link on page 43)—it shows a young man's brain lighting up like a pinball machine while watching the *Avatar* trailer.

NO SPIELBERG NEEDED: 'DO IT YOURSELF'

Fortunately, you don't have to be a big-budget film director to create great storytelling. Smart business leaders understand that what makes a compelling movie work can also drive their marketing. One of my favorite examples is a two-minute video made by GoPro, the pioneering company that made individualized video recording possible for all of us willing to strap a small camera on our head (or arm or ankle or Labrador Retriever).

In the short film, *Fireman saves kitten*, GoPro took actual footage from Fresno firefighter Cory Kalanick's rescue of a kitten from a house fire and turned it into a complete hero story. The video, the majority of it shot from Kalanick's own GoPro, mixes in the audio from the firefighters' radio chatter throughout its two minutes and constructs the story using a classic technique that illustrates a central marketing fact: We wouldn't be able to see the rescue without the GoPro that Kalanick wore that day.

Kalanick's rescue illustrates an important concept we'll learn to apply in this book: *synaptic shortcuts*. For decades, the storyline of firefighters rescuing kittens has been a recurring theme in pop culture. No explanation is needed because we instantly recognize it. It's been part of children's books, it's been made fun of in films such as *Pleasantville*, and now, in GoPro's hands, it's refreshed because of the product's ability to provide a true "you are there" point of view experience.

What do all of these examples share in common? It's that story is the only self-contained communication strategy. The classic storylines are self-contained because they require little or no explanation. You don't have to be a Biblical scholar to know the story of David and Goliath—it's permeated our culture. The idea of the little guy overcoming all odds and knocking off the big guy is an example of a classic storyline that requires little explanation.

As we learned at the very beginning of this chapter, all we needed to move hearts and minds was a storyteller, an authentic story that resonates and an audience. The fMRI gadgetry was nice to demonstrate what was happening, but it didn't make the prom story work. The storyteller and audience had all they needed for a great storytelling experience inside their brains.

Science demonstrates that a great story requires no slide deck, no visual aids, and no gimmickry for success. In fact, a slide deck and visual aids might lead to the reaction Bill Clinton got at the 1988 Democratic Convention. Chances are you've had this reaction to a slide show presentation, even if the slides were glitzy.

When it comes to efficiency, cost and effectiveness, traditional advertising can't begin to match the advantages of story. All you need is an authentic story, ideally one that is a variation on a storyline or archetype that your audience already knows—and knows so well that the audience *anticipates* the next development in the plot.

For all of these reasons, today's gold standard for communication success is *story*.

Considering the science, the mythology and the business examples of storytelling in this chapter, what can you learn that might apply to marketing your own products or services?

- Using story as a strategy is *science*, not a gimmick.
- Story works because it is part of our primitive biology.
- For storytelling to work, it has to reach that deep level where it connects with our collective memory.
- If we can tap into the collective human memory, we can capture attention and engage our prospects.
- Classic storylines can become "synaptic shortcuts," a powerful tool to create real conversations with prospects.

If you were to use story as a marketing strategy, what benefits could you expect?

You can unlock success even when your prospects aren't thinking about it. When you share an authentic story using synaptic shortcuts, you engage those you most want to reach in ways that fully involve them in your story, tapping the biological wiring in their brains. No batteries required!

As you can see, traditional advertising fails at authentic storytelling. How can this be? Advertising is a well-established, multi-billion-dollar global industry. What about traditional advertising could possibly be so wrong? Let's find out in the next chapter.

The story of Carl and Joe

This is a story of Carl and Joe. I don't know if Carl and Joe ever met, but they were certainly fellow travelers. Their shared passion: storytelling.

Carl is Carl Jung, the brilliant psychoanalyst. Joe is Joseph Campbell, the mythologist who gave us *The Hero With a Thousand Faces* and several other seminal works on storytelling and myth. What do these two men have to share with us about storytelling? Everything.

Jung, a contemporary of Sigmund Freud, believed in the mystical power of seminal human stories and in the shared experiences those stories encapsulated, a phenomenon he called the collective unconscious.

Campbell, one of the most famous academics to not earn a PhD, used a faculty lack of approval to continue his studies as the spur for intense self-study that led to an exploration of world cultures and religions and an eventual realization that throughout time, regardless of a society's economic attainment, sophistication or reach, we have told the same stories over and over and over again to educate, entertain, inform and motivate each other.

For 21st-century communicators and marketers, Carl and Joe revealed the secrets of the most powerful kinds of stories we can share.

For Carl, practicing psychoanalysis in Switzerland at the intersection of Europe as World War I erupted around him, the realization was similar. Through his practice, Jung discovered that despite differences in language, culture or ethnicity, his patients all had the same nightmares and dreams.

Jung came to call these stories archetypes, or basic story outlines that we tell ourselves over and over. Examples include the wise old man, the great mother and the trickster. When you read these words, they evoke images of stories you may have read or seen on stage, in film or maybe even experienced in your own life. The archetypes are universal shorthand for an entire story.

In Joe's case, the prototypical powerful story came to be known as the hero's journey, or the Monomyth. In a lifetime of scholarly and entertaining works on storytelling and mythology, Campbell distilled practically every great story to a narrative that today we understand from pop-culture examples such as *Star Wars*.

For Joe, Carl's works were an inspiration and a confirmation of his research. He edited the first papers from Jung's annual Eranos conferences on psychiatry and helped the philanthropist Mary Mellon found the Bollingen Foundation's Bollingen Series of books on psychology, anthropology and myth. Many of Carl's books would later be published in this series.

In what Jung and Campbell wrote, we can identify as many as 12 or 13 distinct character profiles or storylines that we tell in the 21st century. For now, let's focus on just one, a hero story known as the outlaw.

Any aficionado of the *Star Wars* films and Luke Skywalker, or the Dirty Harry movies, will immediately understand this storyline. A simple version goes like this:

- Disgruntled hero doesn't want to be a hero (maybe he's even an outcast)
- Shunned by his or her society, he or she leaves town or heads into the wilderness

- In the wilderness, the hero meets a magic man or woman who teaches him or her some trick, eternal life truth, etc.
- Crisis befalls the hero's society. A villain threatens its very existence.
- The outcast, now a powerful change agent, returns to save his or her society and truly become a hero.

For the film series *Star Wars*, creator George Lucas worked with Joseph Campbell to come up with his ideas about Luke Skywalker the reluctant hero, Yoda the magic creature, the Force, Darth Vader the villain, etc., etc.

The Monomyth: a story above all others?

In his 1949 work, *The Hero with a Thousand Faces*, Joseph Campbell argued that all great stories could be distilled to one basic narrative, *The Hero's Journey* or *The Monomyth*. Campbell offered this definition of what he considered the story above all stories:

A hero ventures forth from the world of common day into a region of supernatural wonder: fabulous forces are there encountered and a decisive victory is won: the hero comes back from this mysterious adventure with the power to bestow boons on his fellow man.

I've reproduced on page 42 an excellent visual depiction of the Monomyth or Hero's Journey, which depending upon the scholar who's interpreting Campbell, might have as many as 17 steps. This one is much simpler yet gets the point across.

There's no doubt in my mind that when we consider storytelling and its application in marketing or any other field, we have to go back to Campbell for understanding (and inspiration). I'm not as certain that there is only one human story to be told.

Nearly four decades in various aspects of storytelling—journalism, public relations, etc.—have given me ample evidence that many, many stories define the human existence. These stories are the fuel that can help you drive success for your company.

In other words, while there's plenty of evidence in human history to demonstrate that stories follow certain steps (character development, a problem, conflict, rising resolution, etc.), there's also a great deal of evidence that there are many stories that define human existence, not just one.

In my view, Campbell came to his conclusion that there is just one story in large part because his work centered on religion and quite often, monotheist religions, those with one god. The similarities in stories he discovered in cultures around the world—the same basic narrative, told over and over, regardless of time, economic achievement or other factors in a society he studied—led him to this conclusion.

When you uncover, develop and share your Capital S Story, you'll find a highly nuanced adaptation of one of the classic story arcs to engage your best-fit clients. It may or may not be the hero's journey, but you don't need to figure that out yet.

The common outcomes of a good Capital S Story answer a question that's central to the success of your organization— why someone should buy from you, or work for you, or invest in you or partner with you. These outcomes are more nuanced than say, a *Star Wars* film, which is a classic example of the Monomyth writ large (with Dolby surround sound, no less).

For our purposes, understanding Campbell's central thesis is an important touchstone as we more fully develop the concept of storytelling, the Capital S Story, and the use of storytelling to engage your best-fit clients.

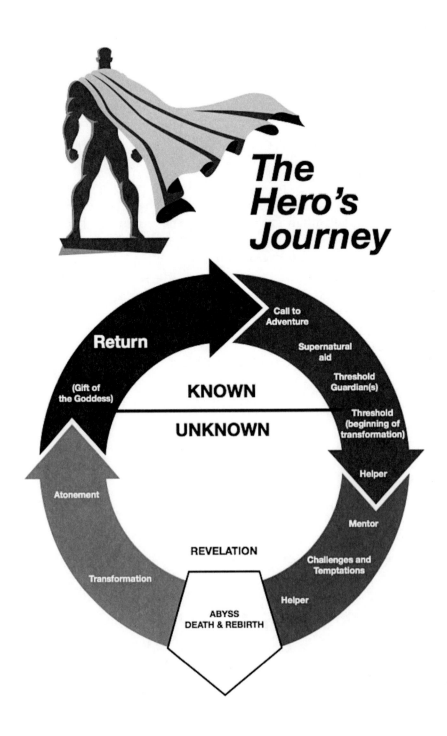

StoryCrafter's Toolkit
Chapter 2

If you're reading the printed edition of the book, access these links and resources through your web browser at: www.capitalsstory.com/storycrafterstoolkit.

If you're reading an electronic edition, just click the links in this box to access all the resources.

- Speaker–listener neural coupling underlies successful communication (the imaging study)
- Actual audio of the story from the study
- Avatar Trailer–Brain Movie YouTube clip
- Why Sharing Stories Brings People Together
- Storytelling in Civic and Political Leadership
- The Secret Weapon That Will Make You and Your Business Stand Out in the War of Ideas

WHAT'S WRONG IN MARKETING TODAY? THE SQUANDERED LEGACY OF JOHN WANAMAKER

Nothing in the muddy, rutted streets of Grays Ferry, Pennsylvania in 1838 seems related to the sound and spectacle we experience in the best-known example of classic advertising, the Super Bowl commercial.

Yet classic advertising probably wouldn't exist today if it weren't for a man named John Wanamaker, born in 1838 in that rural speck that is now part of the city of Philadelphia.

Though Wanamaker's father was a brick maker, John, at age 23, took an entirely different direction, opening one of the first examples of what we know as department stores. From that original store, Oak Hall, to the chain of stores that later bore his family name, Wanamaker's, this retail pioneer transformed the way the world shops—and the way that companies market what they sell. There's something we all can learn from John Wanamaker.

For most of the last 160 years, it seems the advertising industry has remembered only one thing about Wanamaker. It's a quote he supposedly uttered about his pioneering use of advertising: "Half the money I spend on advertising is wasted; the trouble is I don't know which half."

The way most modern marketers use Wanamaker's words does a huge disservice to him, and to the profession these marketers claim to love.

Marketers who spout Wanamaker's quote usually use it as evidence that classic advertising is creative, fun and wild but not very measurable, a field in which "trust me" and "we have no way of measuring that" are common responses to poorly conceived ideas.

This is a ridiculous view. It's one of the reasons why modern marketing has been so disconnected from reality and from real, measurable results. It's also the reason that I believe you shouldn't spend *a single dollar* on your marketing unless you can tell whether that dollar is doing anything for you.

The last person anyone should use to justify lazy or bad marketing is John Wanamaker. Most bad marketers know his quote, but nothing about the man who spoke it.

In the 21st century, the general-purpose department store is in deep trouble, thanks to online shopping and a slew of other changes in our global society. While the department store could soon be gone, it had a good run of roughly 125 years. In 1861, Wanamaker was one of the first to bring the department store to life, changing the way Americans and the world shop.

At the time, the price a shopper paid for any good or service was the product of the kind of haggling that still goes on in ancient bazaars around the world. The idea of a set price for anything was considered a joke or scheme of some sort, until Wanamaker debuted his concept of "one price and goods returnable."

Within a few short years, Wanamaker transformed the retail business as the inventor of what we know today as guaranteed pricing and the money-back guarantee. He also was the first to put music in stores, hiring renowned musical directors, commissioning music and even building theaters inside his stores.

These are defining achievements in the history of marketing. Yet they are not Wanamaker's greatest contribution to classic advertising.

Wanamaker is credited with running the first half-page and full-page newspaper ads, with hiring the first great professional advertising copywriter (after originally writing the ads himself) and with doubling annual revenues from $4 million to $8 million (equivalent to more than $250 million in today's dollars) after hiring his copywriting legend, John Emory Powers.

The combination of Powers, a crank, and Wanamaker, a religious man who wouldn't sell playing cards or advertise in the Sunday papers, set the tone for a tremendously successful marketing run that too many modern-day marketers have forgotten.

As quoted in one history of the early ad business, Powers said he preferred marketing that was really storytelling, essays about certain products: "That was the discovery ... print the news of the store, no 'catchy headings,' no catches, no headings, no smartness, no brag ..."

In other words, Powers preferred authentic storytelling, something that buyers didn't get from most merchants in the late 1800s. Sadly, it's something we still don't get today, even though today's shoppers prize authenticity more than just about anything else in our totally transparent internet world.

The partnership between Wanamaker and Powers led to a kind of long-form advertising (read more about Powers on page 60) that looked much more like journalism, with articles about products, rather than the flash, snap and quick promises that define so much of today's advertising. Storytelling drove the sales by introducing consumers to the products that Wanamaker and his staff had carefully selected.

Along with being an expert marketer, Wanamaker also had a reputation for being honest. Think about that in the context of a field in which modern gurus like Seth Godin write books with titles such as *All Marketers Are Liars*.

What's most disturbing about the way in which many marketers want to use Wanamaker's famous words is that he was committed to measurement and getting results. The difference between the late 1800s and now is that most of what Wanamaker was doing had not been tried before, so there were few benchmarks to use as yardsticks.

In that context, his quote was more about the exciting inability to measure what had not been tried before than it was a glib assertion (as it is today) that a marketer is too lazy or unwilling to measure what works—or that a marketer shouldn't be held accountable for results.

The function of marketing, however creative, is to drive sales and pay the bills. If you run an enterprise where you are paying for cute animal ads and comedy in your advertising, it's great if that's fun, but your advertising is valuable only if it delivers results.

In the 21st century, most companies' marketing messages are right there for analysis on the internet. It's no longer safe to mischaracterize the words attributed to John Wanamaker as a free pass for poorly conceived marketing that may or may not produce results.

That's especially true for business-to-business companies, in which the average sale can be hundreds of thousands if not millions of dollars, and the sales cycle can be months or even years. Businesses need more than a bathroom joke, followed by a wink and a nod to know if their marketing is working. They need measurable results.

For decades, the sexy part of classic advertising for those in the industry has been the ability to chart new creative territory. Far too often, that creative territory has been more about satisfying the egos of those making the ads rather than engaging audiences in a way that delivers bottom-line results for those companies paying for the advertising.

In the 21st century, as our digital world has flattened geographic borders, there is no limitation to creativity in marketing. Creativity is no longer defined by the limits of Madison Avenue. Creativity has become a table stake. A freelancer in Bulgaria could potentially conceive a creative idea equally as unique as someone in one of advertising's iconic agencies on Madison Avenue.

What hasn't changed is what classic advertisers have always owed those paying for the ads: results. On that score, they've historically fallen short, for reasons having nothing to do with serving their clients.

ADVERTISING NOW: FAR FROM WANAMAKER

Advertising as we know it today is a well-established, $600 billion global business. How is it that this business has strayed so far from the ideals of honest and authentic storytelling about products set by Wanamaker and his compatriot, John Powers? We can identify several reasons. Let's take a look.

The rise of Wanamaker's use of advertising coincided with the westward expansion of the United States and the industrial revolution. Across America, as settlers moved west to claim their own piece of promised freedom (and land grants), great industrial minds often led the way or made the way possible. Their creation of modern factories, repeatable manufacturing processes, steelmaking and the engineering and construction of trans-continental railroads could, for the first time in the relatively young history of the United States, take a traveler from sea to shining sea.

As Wanamaker and Powers plumbed the storytelling aspect of the new field we know today as classic advertising, another breed of pioneers experimented with how to move hearts and minds on the frequently wild western frontier.

The success of this pioneer, memorialized in American pop culture as the *snake oil salesman*, is linked with the westward expansion of American railroads. Thousands of Chinese immigrants helped build those railways, and they brought with them traditional medicines, including oils derived from snakes.

The ancient power of these traditional medicines combined on the frontier with the European heritage of the traveling medicine show, and a new genre was born—the "doctor" who traveled from remote western town to western town, often by wagon, sometimes with musical acts or magicians as partners, and frequently accompanied by "cures" in the crowd.

Standing in the midst of the astonished and entertained crowd of Hick Town, these shills extolled the power of the "medicines" being peddled, using audience plants to testify to their magic cures. This is how they encouraged the real townspeople to share in the cure by purchasing their own bottles of the product. The goal of the snake oil salesmen was to huckster enough of their wares to make a quick exit to the next town before their lies were discovered.

At the same time that John Powers began proving the power of storytelling for Wanamaker's in the 1880s, some of the most famous snake oil hucksters were perfecting the power of persuasive lies in marketing.

For example, the Kickapoo Indian Medicine Company, founded in 1881, one year after John Powers joined Wanamaker's, hit the road with customized music composed about its cures. The catchy tunes helped sell sham marketing concepts. So did fake "Indian" ceremonies that were supposed to prove the authenticity of the quack medicines being sold.

The success of medicine shows and "patent medicines" led to displays at the World's Exposition in Chicago in 1893 featuring the dismembering of live snakes, an explosion of newspaper advertising across the country, and the creation of vast enterprises peddling questionable remedies. These enterprises continue today, aided by the power of modern marketing tools such as infomercials and the internet.

As soon as enough of the public woke up to the fakery, the epithet "snake oil salesman" began attaching itself to the field of advertising and to those who practiced it. So the seeds for the deep distrust of many of those who would agree that "all marketers are liars" were sown long ago.

It didn't help that journalists were quick on the heels of the angry public, investigating snake oil salesmen as an era of writers, including Upton Sinclair and Nellie Bly, probed the abuses of meatpacking houses, insane asylums and patent medicines. Their work for the feisty and competitive American press led Congress to pass the 1906 Pure Food and Drug Act that created the FDA, or Food and Drug Administration.

In American pop culture, the popular mob justice practice of tarring and feathering supposed criminals also attached itself to those who considered persuasive lying a key component of marketing. The stain and stench of tar and feathers sadly still adheres to marketing. The continued celebration and practice of lying in 21st-century marketing only ensures that the negative image continues to be an impediment to those of us who see authentic storytelling and fluent storytellers as the heart of true success.

The lingering snake oil epithet is bad enough, but the field of classic advertising picked up even more baggage before it became the field it is today.

As American industrialization and innovation continued, new means of mass communication expanded the opportunities for classic advertising. With the first successful commercial radio broadcast by AM radio station KDKA in 1920, the stage was set for the creation of mass-produced broadcast advertising that could persuade audiences far from the back of any medicine show wagon.

Broadcasting, the American industry that powered our global society's creation of a consumer culture, is a full-throated sensory experience that continues to bring benefits to people around the world. As we will see, advertising made this possible. Advertising also artificially defined the focus of mass communication as a tool to sell products.

While scholars trace evidence of advertising back hundreds of years, there's little doubt that broadcast advertising has largely defined classic advertising as we know it today. And in the infancy of broadcast advertising, there was nothing like what we understand today as a commercial.

In the beginning, broadcasting was a business, yet it was still experimental. Figuring out what to do with it was largely a puzzle. Some thought it could be a great educational medium. Others quickly saw its potential for commercial purposes. Music stores saw that radio could help them sell records and even sheet music. Promoters also used radio to encourage ticket sales for concerts.

It is perhaps part of the American psyche that after we first figure out how to invent something, our second thought as a culture is about how to make money from that invention.

By 1922, shortly after the first radio broadcasts began, numerous businesses, including car dealers and even AT&T, at that time the nation's major telephone provider, were selling radio ads. AT&T later went to court to claim that it should control radio advertising in the same way that it controlled charges for long-distance telephone calls (the company lost of course—imagine if it had won!).

Within a few short years, the creativity and ubiquity of radio and other forms of consumer-focused advertising had captured the popular imagination so broadly that President Calvin Coolidge, in a 1926 speech, declared, "Advertising ministers to the spiritual side of trade. It is a great power that has been entrusted to your keeping, which charges you with the high responsibility of inspiring and ennobling the commercial world. It is all part of the greater work of regeneration and redemption of mankind."

At the same time President Coolidge was elevating advertising to a field focused on bettering people everywhere, clashes over the money to be made from the unregulated field of radio led to a bitter fight in Congress and the passage of the federal Communications Act of 1934.

This law shaped advertising as we know it because it established the Federal Communications Commission. The FCC created rules over the years that say "over the air" radio and TV frequencies are owned by the public and merely leased to private station owners and networks. FCC regulations ultimately required broadcast stations to do educational and public affairs programming for a percentage of the time they were on the air, one of the major ways that broadcasting became more concerned with the concept of time.

This increasing focus on time was supported by the realization of broadcasters that they had to set aside a certain percentage of airtime for "free" or educational and public affairs programming that didn't generate money for them because they couldn't sell ads to support those programs.

From its infancy, broadcast advertising had been focused on how much time to allot for particular programming, including advertising. Over the decades, what we know today as commercials began to take shape in the form of ads designed to fit within 10-, 15-, 30- and 60-second time periods.

This is a huge biological disconnect. There is no scientific evidence that the human brain works best to engage in active comprehension in 10- or 15- or even 60-second segments. That's an artificial construct driven solely by the commercial desire to chunk up air time and create "inventory," or in the broadcast advertising parlance, "space" to be sold to advertisers.

When World War II ended, it was TV's turn to add to the institutionalization of classic advertising as a "creative" endeavor driven by business considerations. The commercial radio networks, well established at this point, became the dominant providers of television content along with their partners in the growing advertising industry. The TV networks applied the same time limitations to television advertising as radio had to theirs.

The pent-up demand of the American consumer, fed by an even more incredible round of industrialization from the American machine that had won the war, was soon powering the growth of classic advertising on the emerging television medium.

ENTER THE MAD MEN AND WELL, MADNESS

By the 1960s, the postwar explosion of broadcast outlets, and the growth of the advertising industry that fed it, had elevated classic advertising to its golden era. In the 1960s, it was just as sexy to be an ad man as it was to be a doctor on one of the daytime soaps paid for by the commercials created by an ad man.

Matthew Weiner's fabulous period drama, *Mad Men*, captures the look and feel of classic advertising's heyday with its inside take on New York City's Madison Avenue, the epicenter of the agency industry in the 1960s.

Mad Men, which ran from 2007-2015, centers on the fictional sexy ad man Don Draper. Draper is the guy so many of us would imagine a classic ad genius to be: a womanizing, hard-drinking troubled soul who somehow creates great advertising while nursing a pounding hangover or dashing from one daytime affair to another, all while looking fabulously crisp in a classic cut suit and white shirt.

Today, the internet is filled with images, memes, quotes and shrines to what the fictional Don Draper said or did or "created" on the show. Most of these shrines have been erected by young people pursuing advertising today. It would be wrong to classify these paeans to an imaginary ad guy as wistful; most of the people paying homage to Don weren't born until the 1980s or later.

What does this tell us? That those practicing classic advertising today—even those who weren't alive during the original era— are looking backwards instead of forwards when thinking about great advertising. Why is this?

CLASSIC ADVERTISING WEARS OUT ITS WELCOME

The 1960s were not only the heyday of classic advertising—they were years of great social unrest. The Vietnam war, civil rights, and other public issues reshaped American culture. The baby boomers questioned everything, and the institution of advertising was no different.

It didn't help that advertising's "greatness" had been built in large measure on selling products, such as tobacco, that were also part of the great public health debates of the 1960s. In 1964, the U.S. Surgeon General issued the first official warning that cigarette smoking was hazardous to health, a move that later led to the banning of tobacco advertising on television.

In addition to selling tobacco, the classic advertising industry was responsible for painting an idealized representation of American consumers and their wants and desires that the 1960s counterculture rejected—the suburban family, led by dad, with mom at home taking care of two kids and driving the wood-paneled station wagon.

In the counterculture, it was easy to tie the advertising industry's glorification of what many saw as social conformity with a history of selling unhealthy products in a kind of social equation that led some to conclude that advertising was still filled with snake oil salesmen. Pushing tobacco made some wonder if advertising needed new attention from something like the FDA.

It's easy to see how some of the historical threads that defined the highly industrialized business of classic advertising, and its celebrated creativity, began to lose their luster—and to set the stage for today's common view that classic advertising is dead.

MILLENNIALS TRUST STORIES, NOT ADVERTISING

Fast forward to our still evolving 21st century, with smartphones, always-on social media, and the technological reinvention of everything. Reinvention ranges from talking smart speakers like the Amazon Echo or Google Home to appliances that talk, like the refrigerators that can be programmed to tell us when it's time to buy milk.

In this era, the classic advertising approach seems both intriguing and irrelevant, like a transistor tabletop radio that you can admire for its classic design while at the same time acknowledging you'll never use it because it doesn't play Spotify or get Sirius XM.

If adding channels or more modern design were all that classic advertising needed to be relevant, all marketers would still be liars. But it's much worse than that for classic advertising and those of us who need marketing to sell the products or services we provide.

Plain and simple, Millennials, the generation born roughly between 1980 and 1996, is now demographically the largest generation ever on the face of the Earth, eclipsing Baby Boomers, that generation born after World War II, between 1945 and 1964.

Globally, there were 75.4 million Millennials in 2016, according to the Pew Research Center, and 74.9 million Boomers. And since the oldest Boomers qualify for retirement and Social Security, age and other factors are catching up with them. In other words, they're dying, and in the next few decades, Millennials will become the dominant generation in the workforce and in deciding what to buy at work or in their personal life. So what Millennials think about marketing and classic advertising has profound implications for all of us who plan to be selling products and services in the years ahead.

By and large, Millennials are the children of Boomers, and like most generations, most of them blame their parents for everything that's wrong with the world, including classic advertising.

In a 2014 study of Millennials by The McCarthy Group, a New York City marketing firm, 84 percent of those surveyed said they don't trust advertising. On a scale of 1 to 5, with 1 being untrustworthy and 5 being completely trustworthy, more than 60 percent of Millennials gave advertising a rank of 1 or 2. They gave a similar rank to salespeople.

The basic sentiments found in this survey have been repeated several times since, depressing news for those of us who seek to market to the world's up and coming decision makers. In other words, we all hate classic advertising.

STORYTELLING RETURNS (IT WAS NEVER GONE)

So what do Millennials (and the rest of us) really like? As *Entrepreneur* magazine put it in 2015, "Millennials Don't Want Ads. They Want Stories." That was the headline on a column by Michael Brenner of a company called NewsCred, in which he reported on his company's study that verified Millennials' distrust of classic advertising.

The NewsCred study also found that "Millennials want to be spoken to like the unique people that they are. Sixty-four percent of the Millennials studied said that they respond more positively to brand messages that are tailored to their cultural interests (music, movies, sports, entertainment), and 62% felt similarly about messages that are useful and help them solve their unique everyday problems."

And what sort of content helps people "solve their unique everyday problems?" It's called storytelling. And of course, this being the 21st century, that storytelling happens, more often than not, online.

One of the most interesting demonstrations of the tangible value of storytelling in business today comes from the Significant Objects (SO) project curated by journalist Rob Walker and Joshua Glenn, author of the book *Taking Things Seriously*.

Over a period of three years, via the auction website eBay, curators and three teams of creative writers repeated a very simple effort. Using powerful stories to describe common auction items, they observed how the application of compelling narrative might affect sales prices.

For example, the storytellers took a hammer-shaped bottle opener and gave it a back story, dubbing its previous owner a 300-pound guy named Mel, who liked to call himself "The Hammer." After spinning an entertaining narrative about this mundane kitchen tool, the bottle opener sold for $40.06 online. (See the sidebar in this chapter for more about Significant Objects.)

The results were astounding, with $128.74 of thrift-store junk selling on eBay for $3,612.51 in the first round of the SO project. The project was repeated two more times, with similar results (and most of the proceeds going to charities).

As Walker and Glenn put it in reporting their results, "Stories are such a powerful driver of emotional value that their effect on any given object's subjective value can actually be measured objectively."

As in, the final sales value being 28 times what was originally paid for the objects! The only difference in why buyers paid so much for what were largely common household objects? The stories told about them in their marketing on eBay.

It's an experiment that's worth seeing to be believed. Melcher Media, producers of the Future of StoryTelling conference, created a great 10-minute video that combines interviews with eBay chief marketing officer Richelle Parham and leaders of the SO project.

Wanamaker and Powers would be proud to know their bedrock commitment to storytelling not only lives in the 21st century, it can now be proven to be objectively effective in reaching today's buyers. Later in the book, we'll explore the importance of authentic stories versus stories that are made up for effect (which critics point out is part of the Significant Objects premise; none of the stories about the Significant Objects had anything to do with reality, they were flights of fancy to see if they would sell mundane goods).

Classic advertising may not be altogether dead, but it's clearly on the way out. Today's buyers have no patience for snake oil salesmen or the industrial era conventions of classic advertising, such as bombastic TV spots or artificially time-limited inventions such as 30-second commercials.

What do today's buyers want? What they always have: Stories. So now it's fair to ask: What's your story? And how will you use it to drive business results?

John Powers, Advertising Storyteller

Reproduced below are two examples of storytelling by advertising legend John Powers, a former journalist discovered by John Wanamaker to help market his department stores. Powers went on to a successful career for many other companies and was inducted into the American Advertising Hall of Fame in 1954. These are examples of his storytelling for the Murphy Varnish Co.

THE COST OF IT.

In a board walk the largest item of expense is the lumber: in a splendid violin the least item of expense is the lumber. In a plain wall the stone is the chief cost: in a piece of classic statuary the cost of the stone is hardly reckoned.

This principle, in a certain degree, applies to the making of fine varnish. We do not pretend that we put from two to five dollars' worth of material into each liquid gallon; but we do put in the scientific knowledge and the expert skill and the long-continued care which no ordinary varnish contains.

If you wish to get rich music or a treasure of the sculptor's art or a job of varnishing that will be satisfactory, you must pay for something else than raw material.   MURPHY VARNISH Co.

THE BEST GOODS

means simply the goods most perfectly adapted to their use. If you wrote your tailor to make up a suit of clothes, on your measure, of his BEST CLOTH, he would not know what to do. He has a dozen cloths that are best for a dozen uses, but you must explain—street suit? dress suit? hunting suit? bathing suit? It makes a difference. Not more difference than the use to which you will put varnish. If you wrote us for a can or a car-load of our BEST VARNISH, we should be as helpless as the tailor. What is it for? That is the first question to settle. A varnish that is perfectly adapted to one use, may be utterly worthless for some other use. Each varnish is made for some particular use, as each cloth is.   MURPHY VARNISH Co.

Image credit: Wikimedia Commons

Significant objects: stories make the sale

This is a fine example of the storytelling employed in the Significant Objects project, reprinted with permission. Original price: $1. Final price: $59. This story by Damion Searls is part one of a five-story teamup with the literary magazine *The Believer*. Proceeds from this auction went to Girls Write Now.

"She had gotten used to the long subway ride, the 3 uptown and past uptown to what came after. She usually saw patients in her office near NYU, but Damien Toussaint was admitted to Mercy's the week of the earthquake and she treated him there, then thought she'd keep seeing him somewhere familiar for their follow-ups after he was discharged.

"His parents lived in Port-au-Prince; both his aunts and all his cousins were visiting from Jakmèl and Les Cayes to help with the preparations for their 40th anniversary. It took three days after the quake to get a call through from New York and find out that the roof had collapsed and killed the whole family. The aunts' houses were undamaged, any other week they and the cousins, who rarely traveled, would have survived. Two days later Toussaint was admitted to the hospital. She and Toussaint didn't talk about his family—there were psychological counselors for that. Her job was physical therapy. He was unable to unclench his shoulders or his fists, the back pain was crippling, he couldn't drive his taxi and couldn't sleep at night except for a few minutes when his body finally collapsed. He woke himself up with the sound of his teeth grinding.

"After his discharge, three weeks later, Toussaint gave her a present. She usually refused these gestures from patients but she could tell it was important to him that she take it, *that he be able to do something for someone. It looked like it came from a 99¢ store but there was something jolly about it, and several times on the long subway ride back she took it out of her purse and looked at it, turning it over in her lap, her face in a frown of what was probably only concentration.*

"She poured the liquid into the bathtub. The lemon scent had a stinging, artificial note—maybe it had spoiled in the years since manufacture? Assuming the little tangerine (pot) still had its original contents, not a refill. Does bubble bath go bad? If artificial lemon scent smells so different from real lemons, why do we perceive it as lemon at all? Her mind wandered. She was tired, she soaped her stomach and breasts, she soaked her sore wrists. She didn't usually take baths after work; it was so she could use her present, it was because of Toussaint's gift. It was his gift. She tried to imagine him happy about it, which was easy, people always like doing something nice. She had a theory that this was the most selfish part about wanting to get married—people marry because they want someone around all the time that they can be nice to.

"After dinner alone in the apartment, she went out. That was the night she met me. I recognized her from the train that day, sitting across from me with a little orange knick-knack in her hand. She was as beautiful all those years ago as she is tonight."

Image of Bubblebath Teapot

StoryCrafter's Toolkit
Chapter 3

If you're reading the printed edition of the book, access these links and resources through your web browser at: www.capitalsstory.com/storycrafterstoolkit.

If you're reading an electronic edition, just click the links in this box to access all the resources.

- Ads You'll Never See Again: 19th Century Snake Oil
- History of advertising: No 96: John E Powers' Wanamaker ads
- 10 Stats That Will Make You Rethink Marketing to Millennials
- Millennials Hate Ads But 58% Of Them Wouldn't Mind If It's From Their Favorite Digital Stars
- About the Significant Objects project
- Significant Objects: Hammer Bottle Opener

4

UNCOVERING **YOUR** GREAT UNTOLD STORY

If the Significant Objects project can multiply the value of ordinary household items 28 times over simply through the power of storytelling, imagine the potential return on investment of storytelling for you and your organization.

Every organization has at least one great, untold story—its own. When I first start working with an organization's leadership, there's frequently skepticism on this point. Early in our work together, we typically talk about the tremendous influence of storytelling on brands such as Nike or Southwest.

So of course, the response is something like, "Well, we're not Southwest" or "we don't have the star power of Nike." To which I usually respond, "Well, you're not an airline or sports apparel company so drop the comparison."

We examine Southwest and Nike elsewhere in this book and in our storytelling work with clients because they are great examples of storytelling that are well-known to most leaders of organizations. They are motivational examples, no different than the poster of a favorite athlete, author or leader you might have hung on your bedroom wall for personal motivation during your teenage years. These examples are like the North Star, they point us in the right direction. We're not going to copy their story. We are interested in *your* organization's story.

When we say every organization has at least one, great untold story, we're talking about the story of your organization, not somebody else's story. This can be hard for an organization's leaders to see. Chances are that they believe their company, its service and products have high value, but that their story is ordinary, uninteresting and unrelated to moving forward successfully.

All three of those things are untrue. If you believe them about your own organization, you are selling yourself and your organization short. And you are denying a true source of your success.

People are interested in authentic stories, even when the subject of the story seems ordinary. We all live in the ordinary, and we care about others who dwell there with us. Consider the long-running success of the TV show *Seinfeld*, which branded itself as a show about nothing but was really a smart take on ordinary life. If you doubt *Seinfeld* has relevance for you, consider the work of a college professor and a photographer.

During my long journalism career, I eventually wrote more than 10,000 stories of various types and later, as an editor, sharpened the impact of at least another 10,000. But it all began with my first journalism class at Miami University of Ohio, taught by Professor John Lowery.

Lowery taught the thousands of us who were privileged to sit in his classes many principles that followed us into successful careers. One of the first and most memorable: Every person has a story worth telling.

Woe to the budding journalist who dared to suggest during professor Lowery's class that some folks just weren't interesting or didn't have a story worth telling. As soon as that smart aleck could grab a pen and a spiral-bound reporter's notebook, professor Lowery had his or her butt out of the classroom and out on the university quad with stern instructions: "Don't come back until you interview someone and bring back the story. And I don't care how long it takes."

Professor Lowery's dramatic exercise, repeated thousands of times and always a great conversation starter at alumni gatherings, also affirms our basic principle: Every person, and every organization, has at least one story worth telling.

Don't believe professor Lowery, despite his decades as a working reporter and additional decades mentoring journalists who've gone on to write and report for major news organizations including the New York Times and CNN?

Then consider a 21st-century example that makes its case through social media success.

In 2010, photographer Brandon Stanton was looking for a new way to bring his art to life. He conceived a project he called Humans of New York (HONY), in which he would photograph 10,000 ordinary people in New York City and plot the locations of their photos on a map.

Stanton decided to include quotes and short statements along with his photos when he posted them on social media, and then, he started posting lengthier stories as blogs accompanying the photos. The stories provoked strong reactions and his followers on social media told Stanton they wanted more and longer stories to go with his remarkable portraits. As soon as he did this, HONY took off.

Today, HONY has 18 million followers on Facebook and 700,000 followers on Twitter. Brandon Stanton's first book-length compilation of HONY stories was a *New York Times* bestseller and spent 31 weeks on the list, twice rising to the number one spot in sales.

HONY has spawned dozens of imitators and has been employed to raise millions of dollars for charity. From the streets of New York, Stanton has taken his camera and his concept to Iran, Peru and other global destinations. Wherever he travels and whoever he photographs, Stanton brings home the same message I first learned in professor Lowery's class: Everyone has a story worth telling—their own. Here's just one example from Stanton's online collection:

"When my wife first told me that she was pregnant, I couldn't sit down. I wanted to rearrange the furniture or something. There was this urgency. Like I should be doing more. My daughter is eleven months old now, and the feeling hasn't gone away. Everything seems so consequential. I've been thinking about everything from her point of view. The memories she'll have in the future are going to be based on the decisions I make now. I especially worry about space. We live in a tiny apartment, and she's got this little 5x5 piece of carpet that she plays on. Today she walked for the first time, using her little pushcart thing. But she can only walk four feet before she hits a wall and has to turn around. And I don't ever want her to feel limited or boxed in. But we looked at new apartments recently, and everything we can afford is so small. So I need to focus. I need to learn more. I need to get a promotion. Because I don't ever want her to have an awareness of being poor. Or any kind of worry at all. I just want everything to feel natural, so she can prioritize her own life and her own feelings."

FIND **YOUR** GREAT UNTOLD STORY—MY PATH

What's true for journalists and photographers is true for organizations, big and small. Companies that understand the power of their story can use that story to attract and engage their best-fit clients. The point of this chapter is quite simply this: You don't have to be a mega company or have a dramatic history for this to be true. You just have to understand some things about story, and how your story is your greatest marketing asset.

I should know. I spent 20 years in journalism before I entered the marketing and PR world and I've spent about as much time in this business since.

While not a guaranteed mint maker for bestselling authors, 20 years in journalism, from trade magazines to daily newspapers to covering the White House and beyond taught me what it takes to uncover, develop and share a great story in our modern world.

There are a few reasons for this: First, journalists are trained critics, oftentimes, skeptics. By education and experience, the good ones cultivate a sensibility about the legitimacy of a good story, about the person or persons sharing the story, and about the story's relevance to the people who matter, which for our purposes, we can call the audience.

Journalism is also great training in the technique of the craft. There is nothing like the repetitive pressure of a deadline to compel a good writer to continually explore the boundaries (and the familiar pathways) that create a good story.

My own early career was spent in two reporting jobs in which I probably wrote the equivalent of five novels worth of words, though I wouldn't paste them together and call them art.

During six years at the Cincinnati Enquirer, the morning daily in that great city, I would write anywhere from three to six stories a day, varying in length from 200 words to 2,000 words (usually a Sunday story of an in-depth, investigative or feature nature). At the Enquirer, I cut my teeth (and skinned my writing knees) rotating through beats ranging from an outlying county seat (Hamilton, Ohio) to the Cincinnati cop shop and municipal courts, to city hall, to county government and special projects (including an investigation of DUI payoffs and of sexual abuse of children by workers at a county home for sexually abused children).

My Cincinnati Enquirer experience buried me deep in the mechanics of sharing the stories of life that most of us take for granted. Few of us (yes, even journalists) want to see ourselves as the subject of a newspaper story. It's just a fact of life that far too many stories in the news are unhappy and no one wants to be at the center of an unhappy story. Yet it's the drama and the dimensions of these stories that sketch the outlines of what really matters to us in life: birth, death, marriage, divorce, success, failure, happy times, sad times.

Why do the Humans of New York stories fascinate us? In part, it's because they're authentic, and they provide meaning from the same kind of dramas—happy and sad times that define our greater purpose.

One of the reasons that classic advertising has failed us so is that the stories spun in some storyboarding session bear so little relation to this kind of drama.

It's phenomenally important to understand the meaning of stories to our lives if you hope to glean something important about the meaning of "story" to successful business communications.

Later, I spent half of my six years at the Washington, D.C. bureau of Thomson Newspapers (now Thomson Reuters) constructing stories for 115 daily papers across 32 states. At Thomson, the task was to take Washington news (which has only become more irrelevant and sillier since I left D.C.) and make it relevant and meaningful to people who lived their lives in small towns across America, a territory we came to call Thomsonland.

At the bureau, this could mean writing up to 15 versions of a story a day, taking a new report on federal assistance to rural airports, for instance, and culling the important details for each community that I was tasked to represent. Or it might mean digging into all the financial disclosure reports of every member of Congress and the Senate for dozens of communities in however many states I wrote for (usually three to six) and explaining what was buried in those dry documents and why it mattered to the daily lives of the people back home.

These two formative experiences, working alongside talented colleagues and for demanding, yet caring editors, helped me to develop a deep understanding of the craft of writing. Early in my journalism career, a mentor imparted this wisdom: Good thinking is good writing. I would add to this tablet-worthy writing maxim that good thinking produces great stories and great stories deserve great writing.

And this brings me to my third point about the relevance of journalism to understanding story as a concept: Executing stories in 200- or 2,000-word lengths is more akin to cutting the stone for the cathedral than it is to envisioning the finished work of art.

In this regard, too many journalists are the deadline-addicted equivalent of Terrell Owens, the often-troubled former NFL wide receiver whose every thought (on life as well as football) seemed to be a variation on "Throw me the ball!" In journalism, every star reporter is a wide receiver running a route—he or she wants to be the star, to get the front-page byline, to write the wittiest sports column, to pen the editorial that puts the mayor in his place. This means that most of those who toil as journalistic storytellers see the field from only one position and one perspective. Their view of the game is singular and might best be described as the *small s* story view of events. Though there are many journalists who work hard to "see the whole field," the truth is that most journalists see only a part of what we might call the *big S* story, or in this case, the big picture.

My ten years as an editor in journalism taught me this important distinction. The job of an editor is to see the whole field, to envision all the routes that receivers run. It's more akin to that of the quarterback or the coach. When I was the deputy bureau chief at the Thomson bureau in Washington, I had daily responsibility to work with my talented colleagues, the regional correspondents, on determining the *small s* and *big S* stories. As you might expect, given America's fractured politics, the big story of the day for a Texas community was not the same as the big story of the day for a community in California. But the federal budget deficit (yes, we had one of those 25 years ago) was a *big S* story that hung over every *small s* story on which community wanted how much money from the federal government for whatever local project.

Later in my journalism career, as the editor of the *Pittsburgh Business Times*, a weekly business journal, I came to see the *big S* story in terms even more clearly. Right or wrong, simplistic or not, we tend to view stories in political life in win/lose, good/bad terms, even though any good journalist will tell you that a story always has more than just two sides. In business, the shades of gray are often far more nuanced and the meaning of the story can be that much more difficult to discern. This is a great problem because far too many journalistic stonecutters keep cutting small little business story pieces while ignoring the *big S* story. This is how we get instant reporting on the ups and downs of the stock market via our smartphones, whipsawing commerce and our personal portfolios on the inanities of the day while ignoring scandals like Bernie Madoff and his ilk.

The *big S* story requires context, meaning and perspective. As an editor of a business publication, I got to know a business community and its leaders in a far more personal and contextual way than someone assigned to cut journalistic stories of 350 words or 15 column inches. Context makes for great stories that transcend the daily headlines; they also fit with our biology and culture as humans, another concept we'll explore later in this book. In journalism, we used to call this the WHOGAS test, a swell acronym for "Who gives a shit?" If a story couldn't meet that test, it wasn't much of a *big S* story. I mean really, speaking as one who wrote too many of them, how can you tell one school board or sewer board story apart from all the others? If I was writing them and couldn't tell the difference, how were my readers supposed to make sense of them?

In the marketing world, we have the slightly more palatable, WIIFM test, the acronym for "What's in it for me?" This presumes a little bit more of a selfish interest than I see in many situations, but it's still a decent test for context.

Meaning may be a bit harder to define. I would argue this is a good thing. If all stories actually have more than two sides, then meaning has more than two definitions. What a grand notion in an always-on, always connected 21st-century world that's seeking transparency. I would argue that one of the reasons that traditional journalism and traditional marketing are failing today is because of their inability to see the world and experience the world as real people do—with the subtle meaning that comes from acknowledging and incorporating more than one or two sides in the larger story narrative.

That brings us to perspective. I learned in my years as an editor, in both working with talented storytellers and the subjects of their stories, that being able to appreciate multiple sides to a story, while not necessarily agreeing with them, deepened the credibility of the narrative and enhanced the willingness of the audience to engage with the story. The richness of life as we know it on this planet does not slide neatly into just two columns or fill just two boxes. It's a sad disservice if our journalism and our business communications fail to represent this richness in the stories we share.

If we fail to incorporate context, meaning and perspective, we paint pictures lacking in the full hues of the rainbow. We tell stories that ring hollow and empty because they lack the voices of the full orchestra. And we share experiences that feel wrong because there is a missing something that doesn't connect with our audience on an elemental, physical level.

Sadly, what I've discovered in my decades in public relations is that the lessons I learned in the journalistic trenches are similarly lacking in the marketing and public relations world.

The same me-centric sensibility infuses the minds of most of those who claim to understand the cool kid businesses of advertising or branding or any other flavor of marketing. Most of these practitioners are great stonecutters. They can cut you a tag line or draw you 15 variations on a logo. But I would hesitate to call either of those branding. And they certainly do not describe what is legitimately called your Capital S Story, especially if you are a large institution or company, and most especially, if you are a company that sells large or complex ideas, products or services to other companies.

A funny commercial with three unshaven 30-something guys acting like emotional 12-year-olds may seem like a great tactical (and maybe even award-winning) way to sell beer, but it's hardly representative of the full context of a particular brewer's story, unless we can agree that all beer is the same and all brewers are the same and all 30-something men act like the same emotional 12-year-olds (at least in award-winning advertising).

Of the 3,000 or so press releases that flood the major press release wires on the internet each day, do the hyper-infused, hyphenated adjectives that fill 2,900 of them really tell the Capital S Story of their "cutting-edge" or "market-leading" product or service? The tumbling stones of cookie-cutter press releases and overused adjectives provide no more context or meaning than the tiny sewer board stories I used to write and edit years ago. They add noise to the environment, making it harder to understand what's important, not easier, yet the PR stonecutters keep churning them out, clogging our minds and obscuring whatever meaning might potentially exist for the audience to appreciate and then engage with in a meaningful way.

And this leads me in the end to ask the biggest question about the application of story in business communications: Are those paying the advertisers, marketers, PR professionals and others willing to appreciate the value of perspective in sharing their stories? If marketing in the 21st century is only going to be about me and my product and my company and my organization and what I want and maybe sometimes what's in it for you (as I define what's in it for you), then how can we incorporate the perspective that our audiences want and need—because of biology and culture—into the stories that we share?

To put it another way: How can we move from commercials that no one believes to stories that allow our ideal clients to "track" with us the way we "tracked" with the young woman telling her prom story in Chapter Two?

My 20 years in journalism and nearly as much time in marketing and public relations taught me that the answer to this question lies in providing an authentic story, rooted in the facts, shared by fluent storytellers who continually read the audience to ensure that engagement is happening and that the audience is part of the story.

Authenticity, fluency and engagement. Three simple concepts—applied far too infrequently. Why is that?

AUTHENTIC STORIES, FLUENT STORYTELLERS AND AUDIENCE ENGAGEMENT: WHY IT MATTERS

Human history illustrates that successful stories rely on these essential elements.

Like the sides of a triangle or the legs of a stool, if all three elements aren't present, the story will wobble or even collapse completely. We've seen this borne out again and again in our work with clients.

Let's take a look at each element.

AUTHENTICITY

Some journalists like to say there are two sides to every story. This is a gross oversimplification. In practically any story—fictional or drawn from life—there are usually far more than two sides driving the narrative. This means there are far more versions of a story than "he said, she said."

Think of your own company. There's your perspective as the leader, those of your managers, employees, customers, perhaps investors, suppliers and neighbors. If you're in a business that has a lot of regulation, you also have regulators. Each one of these categories of "actors" plays a role in your story, and each has a point of view that adds color to the overall picture, voices to the narrative, or additional experiences that, when woven together, make your story unique.

In this context, authenticity means sharing the honest perspective of those involved in your story. Those who work for you, buy from you or supply you become a unique combination of participants in your story—they make your story truly different than any other.

In sharing your story, authenticity does not mean (as superficial journalistic narratives would have it) that there are only two views represented: the hero who's right, and the villain who's wrong. Certainly, your story has heroes and villains—it also has much more than that.

Let's think about a commonplace event that could happen to any of us. If you and I are on street corners at opposite sides of a crowded intersection, and we witness a minor fender-bender, we see the same event, but from different perspectives. I may tell the police one version of what happened based upon what I saw; you may tell a different version because of where you stood. Am I right and you're wrong? Are you right and I'm wrong? It's rarely that clear in life, whether we're talking about a fender-bender or your company's unique story.

Authenticity means that your great story reflects the views of all the participants—what they see, what they have to say, what they feel. This is what makes it truly unique. For a few years, communications agency Cohn & Wolfe did an annual survey of companies valued by consumers for their authenticity. In the firm's 2017 edition of the annual survey of more than 15,000 consumers, Amazon came out on top.

As one of the world's largest and most successful corporations—owned by the richest man in the world, Jeff Bezos—Amazon is a perfect illustration of our concept. There are many views on Amazon, its impact on society, good or bad, and on the world economy. Whether it's the company's announcement a few years ago that it might use drones for local delivery, or the enormous competition in recent years for Amazon's so-called HQ2, a second headquarters that promised up to 50,000 jobs, it's clear that Amazon is a company whose story elicits multiple views. It's not a two-sided story; like most in life, it's a many-sided story.

A FLUENT STORYTELLER

How many times have you seen a film that had all the right actors, all the right potential storylines, and yet, when you left the theater after the final credits rolled, you were disappointed by the way the story was told?

How often have you sat in a meeting, excited by the prospect of the project at hand, only to be sorely disappointed after the "leader" shared his or her vision of the project?

We can relate the same emotional experience to a book we bought, a vacation experience we tried, even a political candidate we voted for, that didn't turn out to be what we thought.

In great disappointment, we shake our head and wonder how the individual filmmaker, author, leader, etc. let us down when they had such great material. The answer is simple yet not obvious until we put it into a storytelling context: Not everyone is a fluent storyteller.

How does this play out when we're talking about a story that's designed to attract your best-fit clients?

The most common mistake I see in our work is that potential and actual clients pick their storytellers by where they sit on the organizational chart rather than by taking a look at their authentic contribution to the company's story (see the authenticity section a couple pages back).

The best example of this would be a tech company where it's immediately assumed the CEO should share the story of the innovation or product driving the company. Yet that's often the wrong approach. Very few tech companies are led by CEOs who are both visionary inventors and great communicators. You don't find someone like Apple's Steve Jobs at every company.

In the case of many tech companies, especially those with revolutionary innovations or products, the leader who can build the organization that can bring the idea to market may not be the most fluent storyteller. That job might better be handed to the inventor who came up with the crazy idea that is now so marketable. It's the inventor who can share the heroic initial struggle of trial and error that led to the brainstorm and creation of the innovation or product.

Think about your own organization, and think again about the collection of actors who make your story unique. You don't have to run a tech company to understand that fluent storytellers can live in many areas of your organization outside of the C-Suite.

If you run a manufacturing company, your story might best be shared in some circumstances by having that long-term shop foreman retrace his 30-year history with the company and how he has personally worked to make the product or company the success it is today. In a health care setting, it might be the nurse on the floor who's delivering care in YOUR organization rather than another because of your unique story and her ability to play a part in that story.

Think about this in context to what we considered earlier: the objection that your organization doesn't have a great story because it isn't Nike or Southwest Airlines or even Apple.

When I'm buying machine parts or seeking high-risk health care, the last thing I want is a mercurial visionary and revolutionary like Steve Jobs trying to sell me something. I want the reassurance of that foreman who can trace every dip and curve on a gear spline I want to buy, or the nurse who can go beyond medical competence to comfort me in a time of trouble by sharing how I've chosen the right health care provider because of the values that drew her to work there.

We'll dig deeper into the development of your fluent storytellers later. For now, all we need to remember is that you need more than an authentic story with the right ingredients. You need someone who can fluently share that story.

And that brings us to the third and most often forgotten element of a great story: the importance of your audience and your role in keeping them engaged.

READING THE AUDIENCE

A great story and a fluent storyteller won't do you any good if you're sharing that great story with passion in front of the wrong audience.

One of my favorite examples of poorly reading the audience comes from the 1980 movie, *The Blues Brothers*. In one scene early in the movie, the Jake Blues character played by the late

John Belushi "appropriates" the country gig of another band, lying to his bandmates and the bar owner about the country chops of his band so that the band can play.

As soon as the band cranks up *Gimme Some Lovin'* by the Spencer Davis Group, a 1960s R&B standard with driving bass and soaring horns, the Blues Brothers band discovers why there's chicken wire between the bar and band, as the crowd at Bob's Country Bunker starts hammering the screen with beer bottles and other glassware. In a moment of desperate inspiration, the Elwood Blues character played by Dan Aykroyd suggests the band play the theme from the TV series *Rawhide*, and the crowd loves it.

This funny and somewhat flip example illustrates the point that you have to do more than know your audience. You have to engage that audience. In our work with prospects and clients, we find time and again that storytelling fails when there isn't a connection with the audience.

Early in my public relations career, a CEO of a very large public company pointed to a front-page *Wall Street Journal* story about a competitor and said to my PR team, "Get me this story." Why did the CEO want this story? Because he hated his competitor, felt he was more deserving of the front-page of the *Wall Street Journal* and he had an ego. Now, getting exactly the same story about his company in the same news outlet that covered his hated competitor might have been a good idea for the CEO's company—or he could have found himself taking the journalistic equivalent of hurled glassware from some of the best reporters in the business at the most respected business publication in the world because they'd already written that story.

The CEO wanted to be in the *Wall Street Journal* for all the wrong reasons. He may have assumed that his stakeholders read the paper. Just because his competitor had a story in the paper didn't necessarily mean it was so, however. And he really couldn't articulate how a story in the *Wall Street Journal* would keep his stakeholders engaged as he shared the company story.

In the 21st century, because of the internet, we can measure whether your audience is engaged. The metrics available to do this don't change the basic principle that a great story needs an engaged audience—they just uncover the metrics that prove this is the case.

Here's another example that predates the internet a bit and proves the case: The Three Tenors. This union of opera stars Plácido Domingo, José Carreras and Luciano Pavarotti took opera out of stuffy opera houses and put it in soccer and football stadiums, leading to hit albums, a world tour and exposure to new audiences (see box). Instead of bemoaning declining traditional audiences for their flavor of classical music, the tenors sought out new audiences in new places and found success.

Engaging your audience is the element that ties successful storytelling together. You might be the finest opera singer the world has ever known, but if you're singing to the wrong audience in the wrong place at the wrong time, the world will never get to know you—and you may be wearing shards of glassware like Jake and Elwood Blues.

In my experience, making sure the audience is engaged is both the most important—and most often forgotten—element in the recipe for great storytelling success. The best storytellers, whether famous or not, understand that this is a continuous dance, much like the Princeton storytelling experience we learned about in chapters one and two. Remember the fMRI images, which showed the brain activity of the storyteller *and* the listener responding to each in a kind of storytelling choreography.

Now that you understand you don't have to be Nike or Southwest Airlines to have a great untold story, you can begin to uncover your own story.

And now that you understand the three critical elements of successful storytelling, you are undoubtedly asking: How can I put these together for my organization?

Let's start to answer that question by explaining how I got here and how the WordWrite story brings these principles to life.

If it sells tickets, is it still opera?

The famed opera singer José Carreras was recovering from leukemia in 1990 when his friend Plácido Domingo had an idea: What if he and fellow tenor Luciano Pavarotti celebrated their friend José's recovery by joining together for a concert?

They billed themselves as The Three Tenors, and their first concert benefitted the José Carreras International Leukemia Foundation. As stars in the relatively small world of opera, The Three Tenors could hardly have predicted that their goodwill gesture would create a multimillion-dollar business that brought opera to millions of new listeners over the better part of two decades.

The Three Tenors experience is a remarkable illustration of our third storytelling principle, the one that most organizations fail to achieve: continually reading the audience in a way that keeps them engaged.

When The Three Tenors held their first concert, they weren't thinking about introducing opera to new listeners. Domingo and Pavarotti were just happy that their friend Carreras had recovered from leukemia and would be singing professionally again. The concert was a great success and raised a good sum of money after it was broadcast to a global audience.

Despite that audience reaction, it was four years before The Three Tenors did a second concert, and not until 1996 when they went on the road to make millions and sing opera in dozens of unlikely venues, including Wembley Stadium, more famous certainly for the concerts played there by The Beatles in 1963 and 1965.

Successful storytelling rests on an authentic story, fluent storytellers and the discipline to keep the audience engaged. Opera has given the world some of its most beautiful, authentic music. The Three Tenors are certainly examples of great operatic storytellers. As Carreras said of Pavarotti in one 2000 interview, "Luciano is a born communicator, one of the most charismatic figures I have ever seen on stage. He only opens his mouth and with the first note, he gets the audience."

Yet as an ensemble, it's not the authentic stories of opera or the fluent storytelling of The Three Tenors that made them famous. It's that after their first couple concerts, when new listeners responded to their art, these talented singers decided to keep the audience engaged by taking their authentic art and storytelling talents to new audiences.

In a happy-ending flip side to the *Blues Brothers* example cited in this chapter, The Three Tenors found a way to engage new audiences in what had been, until then, a story shared with very few within the strict confines of opera halls in which music has been performed for centuries in a manner defined by Western European tradition.

The concerts were huge successes, with each tenor eventually earning $1 million for each performance and stadiums filling with 50,000 to 60,000 listeners. For comparison, that's a total that would dwarf the *full season* attendance of most major opera companies.

Along with the concerts came best-selling recordings, including *The Three Tenors In Concert*, which still holds the Guinness World Record for best-selling classical album of all time.

Opera purists bashed The Three Tenors for using amplifiers and other techniques to play their music in football and soccer stadiums. To keep the audiences engaged, the tenors sang more than opera—another decision that drew criticism.

In 1998, Pavarotti dismissed the critics for challenging the group's successful audience engagement: "The purists, they say this is not opera. Of course it's not opera, it doesn't pretend to be an opera. It's a concert in which we sing some opera, we sing some songs, we do some zarzuela, then we do a medley of songs. ... We respect very much when people criticize it. That's fine. They shouldn't come ... But they should leave the people who are coming and are happy."

Whatever you may think of The Three Tenors approach to engaging an audience, that's a worthy question for you in sharing your great untold story: Is your audience happy and engaged?

StoryCrafter's Toolkit
Chapter 4

If you're reading the printed edition of the book, access these links and resources through your web browser at: www.capitalsstory.com/storycrafterstoolkit.

If you're reading an electronic edition, just click the links in this box to access all the resources.

- From YouTube: Seinfeld, the show about nothing
- About Humans of New York
- HONY: The pregnancy story
- The Three Tenors at Wikipedia
- How The Three Tenors Sang The Hits And Changed The Game

THE WORDWRITE STORY:
HOW I GOT HERE

On a forgotten Friday afternoon many years ago, I sat in my office just off the newsroom of the weekly business journal I edited. I held the latest issue of the *Pittsburgh Business Times* in my hands, just back from the printer. It smelled of still-damp ink and the folds of the pages felt crisp and fresh in my hands. The phone rang.

On the other end was Larry Werner, head of the largest PR agency in town, a man dubbed "the prince of Pittsburgh PR" for his long career, sage counsel and deep experience. A few months earlier, facing the prospect of yet another move to yet another city to pursue yet another rung on the journalistic ladder of success (yes, there used to be one of those), I had quietly asked Larry to help me find another job in Pittsburgh. Our kids were young and we had family in the area. We weren't exactly ready to move to Orlando or Sacramento or Wichita, places the company had suggested I might land (though when or where was awfully unclear).

After the pleasantries, Larry got right to the point. "Paul, I'm not going to help you."

The blood rushed to my head. Grabbing the paper, I began leafing through the pages and breathing heavily into the phone. Clearly our paper had written some story about a client that had angered the Pittsburgh head of Ketchum Public Relations, the most prestigious PR shop in town, the founding office of the fifth-largest PR firm in the world.

After what seemed like 10 minutes of silence, Larry spoke: "Well, aren't you going to ask me why?"

"OK Larry," I sighed, waiting for the worst. "Why?"

"Because I want you to come work for me, not somebody else."

Well, now that was unexpected! Whatever else you may think of journalists, it is true that many of us have blind spots that could be career killers in other fields. One of mine was exceedingly poor networking skills. It never occurred to me that when you ask somebody to help you find a job, they might actually consider offering you a job themselves.

As much as I had learned in my journalistic career, it took a series of unexpected events, such as my call with Larry, to put me on a path where all my journalistic storytelling experience could actually help someone like you uncover, develop and share your great, untold story.

I spent four years as a vice president at Ketchum Public Relations, working for clients across the country and overseas. From airlines to universities to manufacturers, from big events to product launches to crises, my time at Ketchum was like earning a pinnacle degree in PR.

THE STORYTELLING ENTREPRENEUR

And while my time at Ketchum taught me a great deal about marketing and PR as businesses, it still left me hungry for great storytelling. The firm and its many smart people routinely and repeatedly won awards for the fantastic work they did. Yet something was missing: The focus on the Capital S Story that I had learned to be so important during my years in journalism.

This lack became clear to me in 2002, when another series of events led me to form WordWrite on the bedrock of story.

Along with dozens of my colleagues, I had left Ketchum's Pittsburgh office as the dot.com implosion destroyed ill-conceived tech startups with outrageous names, dragging their PR firms down with them. Once again forced to rely on my inferior networking skills, I started looking for a job at a client company, only to be told repeatedly that this was a stupid idea. That is not a comforting statement for a husband and father with two young children and a mortgage.

Dick Singer, a wise friend who is today my Vistage business coach, asked a simple question when I whined about all this to our regular job networking breakfast group: "Well, did you ask them WHY they would tell you such a thing?"

Well, no—I just kind of took it as an insult until Dick reminded me to ask the question. One meeting in particular stands out. The co-founder of one of the largest agencies in Pittsburgh, a man known for his strong opinions (and the intense dislike many had for them), at first refused to network with me. He crushed my spirit by phone by indignantly refusing to meet and as I was hanging up, I could literally hear his voice trailing off, "No wait!"

"I'll meet with you," he said, "on the condition that you agree to form your own PR agency. I will tell you what you need to do to make that happen. There isn't a PR storyteller as good as you in town, and I dare you to name one."

True to his word, I met with the agency co-founder and he was his irascible, cantankerous self throughout our 30 minutes. He talked. I listened. I wrote down everything he said. Occasionally I would name some PR leading light in town and he would verbally eviscerate them between dictums on how much I should charge clients, when to hire staff, open an office, etc.

Within a month, a neighbor and attorney had gotten me incorporation papers to create a company. I was still chasing a few job leads, and as I sat at home one day in late February 2002, the phone rang and on the caller ID, I could see it was a former Ketchum client who had liked me and gone on to a big job at an international chemical company. Tim really wanted to hire me but I knew he liked to change jobs frequently and take his team with him. I really didn't want to jump on the move-every-few-years train.

"Paul, I've got good news and bad news," he said over the phone. "Which do you want first?"

"I don't know, Tim," I said, "You pick."

"Well, the bad news is that I can't hire you," he said (of course, this was kind of good news to me). "And what's the good news?" I asked.

"If you had an agency, I could hire you tomorrow," Tim said.

"Well, Tim, I am sitting here holding the incorporation papers in my hands," I said, staring up at the heavens to see if this was God's joke.

"Great," he said. "Contact my assistant and make arrangements to be here in New Jersey next week."

I hung up the phone and, as I hummed to myself, the pen flew through the blanks and boxes of the incorporation form. About 15 minutes later, the phone rang again and I looked at the caller ID. Uh-oh. Tim again. Well, there goes that one.

"Paul, there's a problem," Tim said when I answered. "I figured as much," I said, trying not to sound crushed.

"Yeah," Tim said. "It seems that unless you have a business checking account and I can wire you $6,000 a month into your account the first of the month, this isn't going to work." I choked a bit, then laughed. "I think I can make that happen," I said.

Nearly two decades later, WordWrite is still going strong. The conviction—and the experience—of nearly four decades in communications, and nearly two full decades of WordWrite illustrate that when it comes to brand versus story, it's story that wins every time. Story infuses everything we do at WordWrite. And a Capital S Story that's successfully uncovered, developed and shared, leads to the best branding we could possibly imagine.

THE FOCUS THAT LEADS TO YOUR HAPPY ENDING

So, what exactly does that look like? Here are the stories of a few of our clients, organizations not unlike yours, though their size, industry or focus may be different.

YOUR CHAMPION FOR VICTORY

As a teenager, Eric Guy struggled to fit in with the prescribed, limiting structures of school. Difficult family circumstances exposed him to the real meaning of the word "challenge." Eric blended his family and life experiences with an education at one of the nation's finest schools of social work, a powerful combination that led him to create Center for Victory (CFV).

CFV is a team of professionals delivering magnetic programs that produce life-changing results for people and organizations. As the business has grown, so has Eric's realization that CFV can be a powerful force for change on a much broader level. Eric engaged WordWrite to uncover and develop the Capital S Story that would help CFV reach a new level of achievement by better sharing its story. Over several months, WordWrite worked with Eric and his team through our StoryCrafting process to create, develop and share the authentic story of what Center for Victory does, in a way that's easily understood, memorable and engaging.

Once the story was clearly identified, we worked together to map out how best to share the Center for Victory story. The project took four months to complete, in large measure because of CFV principals' lack of availability due to travel. The budget and geography were our greatest constraints. Much of our early work (including qualitative interviews of CFV associates) was done by phone and e-mail. WordWrite's StoryCrafting process involved the following tasks:

Collaboratively, we asked and answered Five Burning Questions about CFV that helped us establish the Center for Victory's Story Fundamentals, including market size, competition, targets, segments and share. The Story Fundamentals are building blocks that helped frame the Center for Victory story. These included separating CFV from its initial focus on social service agencies as clients; focusing on businesses and business leaders as a core audience; and defining CFV in a way that separated it from the plethora of charlatans claiming to provide services similar to Eric and his team.

Answers to the five burning questions also helped us identify the Center for Victory story anchors—the essence of the story that we then matched to a story archetype. An archetype is the effective "shortcut" that helps audiences immediately understand the Center's story. For example, a "David and Goliath" archetype enables an organization to gain quick audience understanding to more quickly and effectively engage its audiences. An archetype is the effective shortcut that helps audiences grasp an organization's story.

The StoryCrafting process led Eric and the CFV team to rethink their story at an elemental level, stripping away professional terminology to reveal the core purpose of the organization. Drawing on WordWrite's proprietary archetype identification process (based on influences including the work of Carl Jung and Joseph Campbell), the CFV team agreed they act as champions—not in the traditional, "I win gold medals" sense, but in the sense of being champions for the individuals and organizations they serve. This iteration of the Champion archetype is derived from elements of the Outlaw and Caregiver archetypes found in classic literature (see diagram on page 101).

After identifying the best archetype, WordWrite worked with Eric and his team to determine the storytelling roles of team members—identifying those who, in addition to Eric, are best suited to tell the overall story or aspects of it. In this case, it was his team of coaches who worked alongside him with clients.

Our final step was to determine the most appropriate strategies to "read the audience" and assure that the sharing of the Center for Victory story is effectively measured through interaction with the audiences the Center reaches (media, prospects, etc.).

The archetype was effectively pulled through to revise how CFV principals talk about the organization in communications, up to and including creation of a new brand identity in a logo and a new tagline, both of which are reproduced here.

The new CFV story and identity was unveiled to unanimous acclaim at a meeting of the CFV team of associates. Since the meeting, the CFV story and identity have been incorporated into all ongoing communications and new channels as well, especially the CFV's social media channels, which have become more vibrant and focused in their messaging, thanks to the StoryCrafting process.

MCCLINTOCK & ASSOCIATES: SAGE ACCOUNTING

The StoryCrafting process helped McClintock & Associates (M&A) establish a central theme about its core "Story" that expresses its culture, values and business essence. As a firm with nationally recognized experience in the highly specialized field of accounting for postsecondary, for-profit educational institutions, M&A had a difficult time expressing its value to clients without lapsing into accounting jargon or citations of obscure federal regulations.

After working closely with M&A staff to uncover the Five Burning Questions that undergird the McClintock Story, WordWrite identified the Sage archetype as a good fit, for at its core a Sage organization is about *wisdom*.

As a firm born from possessing specialized knowledge, its style of client engagement and the rhythm of professional accounting practice, M&A is a "wisdom-centric" organization.

How can an accounting firm act like a shaman or wise hero or sage? Yes, accounting firms seek to be founts of arcane financial knowledge, especially about taxes, but that is considered a table stake—a given. How was M&A different than all the other accounting firms?

The way the firm goes about its daily work involves advising clients in an ethically responsible manner in an industry that's been ethically challenged. So M&A's *application* of its wisdom and its *specialized knowledge* drive success for its clients. These are essential characteristics of Sage organizations.

For McClintock, our work revealed three sage-like characteristics at M&A. These include:

1. A search for "truth" by applying known standards objectively in all cases
2. Aiming for expert status via critical thinking and analysis
3. Achieving expert status via wisdom and self confidence in the firm's area of expertise, an attribute we didn't find in M&A's competitors

When we uncover a client's archetype and adapt it to develop the client's Capital S Story, this is not a linear process. M&A professionals are not waxing poetic about being Sages when they're interacting with clients and prospects. The application of an archetype to a client's Capital S Story is far more nuanced than that.

For example, lots of discussions about "brand" are really discussions about colors and logos and "look and feel" of a company's presence in its marketplace. These are table stakes and unless they represent the company's Capital S Story—they may well confuse stakeholders about the company or worse, be so off-putting as to be wasted expenses.

Don't get me wrong; a company's brand is critically important. To be successful, it must flow naturally from the Capital S Story. It must be the embodiment of that story.

For example, with M&A, we translated the Sage archetype into a brand that would resonate with clients and prospective clients. We didn't slap the word "Sage" on everything and call it a day. Working together, we imbued the Sage sensibility into all the key communication channels comprising the M&A brand platform, including creation of a new brand tagline, *A Higher Grade of Accountants.*

As a result of our collaboration, the McClintock Sage story has been incorporated into all aspects of the firm's marketing, from a new brand identity to the website to social media and even trade show marketing. In just one measure of success, in the first year of our collaboration, web traffic increased by more than 350 percent year over year just by having a better story to share, and by sharing that story through means that the firm's clients and prospects could best be reached.

These are just two examples of the happy endings we've helped clients to craft for their Capital S Stories using our StoryCrafting process. Championing the success of individuals and organizations and providing sage advice to a specialized category of post-secondary educational institutions are two disparate—and I would argue difficult—applications of the idea of storytelling as a successful marketing paradigm. But it's working.

More than anything else, these two examples illustrate that your story doesn't have to be that of a Nike or Southwest to produce great results. Let's take a look at why that's the case in the next chapter.

Archetypes: An overview of the 12 most common characters in storytelling

In this chapter, we've spent a fair amount of time using the word *archetype*. Archetypes came into general use first in literature and psychiatry. Simply put, an archetype in literature defines a type of character we might find in a story. In psychology and psychiatry, archetypes have been used to organize dreams in particular, a practice that began with the psychoanalyst Carl Jung more than 100 years ago (and developed in his book, *The Archetypes and The Collective Unconscious*).

Over the years, as storytelling has gained in prominence in marketing and other fields, many "experts" have tossed around the term *archetype* while applying various meanings to it.

Most approaches to identifying and organizing archetypes reach a consensus that there are about 12 archetypes or characters that might be encountered in literature. In our view, there are many more than that. When we work with clients, we can drill very deeply into a catalogue of hundreds of archetypes.

To keep things simple, in the wheel graphic on page 101, we have adapted the work of Margaret Mark and Carol Pearson, who wrote the book *The Hero and the Outlaw: Building Extraordinary Brands Through the Power of Archetypes*, to create our variation of 12 primary archetypes that we employ in our StoryCrafting work with clients.

While some scholars, such as Joseph Campbell (see Chapter 2), have argued that there is only one kind of story with one kind of hero, our view is that variations on the archetypes described below (plus many others we've developed in our WordWrite StoryCrafting toolkit) can become heroes in their own stories.

Certainly, the prevalence of stories featuring the Jester archetype as hero are much less frequent than other archetypes, but they do exist. Each has its place when describing the Capital S Story of a particular organization.

In the two client examples in this chapter, you can clearly see the Sage archetype we developed with McClintock & Associates accounting firm on this wheel. In some variations of this archetype wheel, this archetype might have another name. It's important to know that this is a hero who has knowledge and shares it.

In our work for the Center for Victory (CFV), we adapted elements of a few archetypes to arrive at the concept of Champion. We crystalized our adaptation in the new tagline for CFV, *Your Champion for Victory*. In our adaptation, CFV is not the classic hero archetype you see on the wheel below—that particular role belongs to clients of CFV, who unlock their true potential through their work with the company.

In our adaptation, we synthesized an archetype that describes an organization committed to bringing out the best in the people and organizations it serves. In this regard, CFV is more of a coach than a classic hero. Elements of other archetypes, including the caregiver and sage, have been incorporated into the development of the CFV Capital S Story.

This archetype wheel is a handy reference for us as we continue on our journey to fully understand why your story drives your brand.

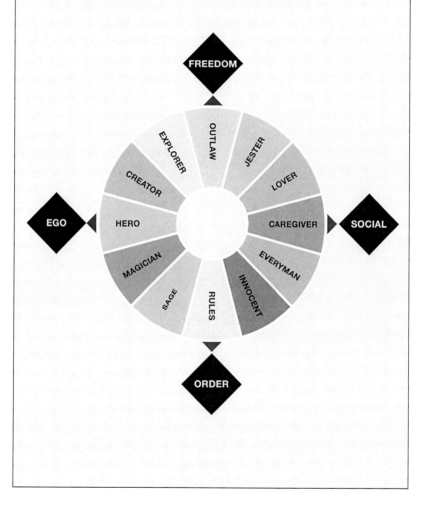

Bringing archetypes to life: a client example

To better understand how the classic concept of an archetype is lived in real life, here are some examples of the Sage archetype WordWrite shared with a client during a StoryCrafting engagement to better visualize the concept.

	Examples of the Sage	Evidence
	Oprah Winfrey: The so-called "queen of all media" single-handedly curates many Americans' interests in books, culture, politics and other areas solely from her status as a cultural advisor.	"Oprah Winfrey is a media titan, philanthropist, businesswoman, fashion icon, actress, and all-around American treasure—and a new museum exhibition is now giving her the credit she deserves." –Glamour magazine
	The New York Times: Even amid radical changes within conventional journalism, this newspaper fulfills a powerful "agenda-setting" role about the issues of the day	"It is among the most influential news organizations in America, playing a distinct role in setting the nation's agenda." –Nieman Lab at

	for America—in culture, politics and other arenas.	Harvard University
	Google: As a company, Google completely altered the manner, depth and detail of how we obtain and process information. It essentially brought the Library of Congress to anyone with an internet browser and some curiosity. Google was neither the first, nor is it the only search engine that drives internet browsing. But unlike its competitors, it has successfully claimed the leading role in defining "the algorithm" as something that grants it Sage status among the public, Wall Street investors and other institutions.	"Google's strength has always been updating its algorithms and experience alongside morphing user behavior. In the sink-or-swim environment of search and online platforms, you can expect to see Google adapt and test new products to compete with these competition points." –Forbes

	**Mr. Miyagi (actor Pat Morita)**: The martial-art mentor from *The Karate Kid.*	"Unassuming, sagacious, slightly secretive—all characteristics of Mr. Miyagi, whom Morita brought to life in four Karate Kid movies." –Entertainment Weekly
	**Warren Buffett**: The American mega-investor who befitting his Sage status in today's culture is often referred to as the *Oracle of Omaha* for his investment prowess.	"Buffett, the Sage of Omaha, Makes Value Strategy Seem Simple: Secrets of a High Plains Investor" –International Herald Tribune

StoryCrafter's Toolkit
Chapter 5

If you're reading the printed edition of the book, access these links and resources through your web browser at: www.capitalsstory.com/storycrafterstoolkit.

If you're reading an electronic edition, just click the links in this box to access all the resources.

- A psychological overview of archetypes
- Scott Jeffrey: The ultimate list of archetypes
- Ariel Hudnall's study of archetypes in fiction
- The Center for Victory website and branding
- McClintock & Associates website and branding

HOW TO UNCOVER YOUR CAPITAL S STORY WITH STORYCRAFTING

As we've learned in the previous chapters, in the 21st century, the classic approach to marketing is no longer delivering the results it once did. Across the industry, ad agencies are consolidating, folding, gobbling up digital shops, in short, seeking some remedy for their ever-shrinking ability to deliver results by continuing to follow their old model.

They don't seem to be grappling with the real reason for their problems: The world in which your organization competes for attention is inundated by competing information and messages. One measure of this comes from a 2015 Microsoft study, reported by TIME Magazine.

According to TIME, "Researchers in Canada surveyed 2,000 participants and studied the brain activity of 112 others using electroencephalograms (EEGs). Microsoft found that since the year 2000 (or about when the mobile revolution began) the average attention span dropped from 12 seconds to eight seconds.

"As a result, the researchers found, 'Heavy multi-screeners find it difficult to filter out irrelevant stimuli—they're more easily distracted by multiple streams of media,'" TIME reported.

This means that the audiences you most want to reach are hungry for meaning, yet they struggle to find it in the sea of information coming at them. As our journey thus far demonstrates, you can provide meaning by sharing YOUR story. But how do you do that?

In the last chapter, I introduced you to StoryCrafting, Word-Write's patented process for uncovering, developing and sharing your organization's great untold story. What makes our process different? And why should you consider this type of approach for your story? Let's look under the hood and find out.

As we often say among us "WordWriters," we're like the chef who eats his or her own cooking. We're not going to ask you to do something that we haven't done ourselves. So let's take a look at how we've employed our own storytelling process to deliver results for WordWrite. What you'll read on the following pages is the result of work undertaken in the last six years or so. Much like our mythical chef, we have returned to our "Storytelling Kitchen" many times to perfect our recipe. We hope you like it.

To help you understand where we're going, let's remember our goal: To evolve the story of your organization so that the story and the organization are seamlessly aligned. To return to food analogies for a minute, we want your alignment to be as clear as this: You don't have to say a steak is food for people to understand that it's something you eat. Ideally, you want your Capital S Story to be that clear. When you share your Capital S Story, your best-fit clients should be able to understand what you do and who you are right away.

To understand what I'm going to share about the WordWrite story and how we developed it, let me first lay out a few principles that will be the signposts on our journey.

THESE PRINCIPLES DEFINE STORYCRAFTING

StoryCrafting focuses on uncovering, developing and sharing what we call the Capital S Story, which expresses an organization's essence. When you uncover your Capital S Story, you learn that it has unique qualities rarely found in classic advertising or marketing. The Capital S Story taps into what defines an organization and harnesses that in ways that are appealing and valuable to the audiences the organization wants to engage. A Capital S Story developed through StoryCrafting is:

- **Unique**: The story belongs to this organization alone—it can't be copied by competitors.

- **Authentic**: In the 21st century, all audiences are skeptical and they all demand an authentic business story. So how you share your story must cut through this skeptical mindset.

- **Driven by a Story Archetype**: Our StoryCrafting process builds on the work done by Carl Jung, Joseph Campbell and others to provide a visceral connection to your authentic story by employing archetypes (see previous chapter). In our experience, a timely, archetype-based story is the most rapid means by which a client "story" can be understood by existing and new audiences. Decades ago, the debate in sales and marketing was focused on whether you should describe "features" of your product or service or "benefits." In other words, should you talk about yourself or your best-fit client? When you share your authentic story, built upon the right archetype, it's not about you or your best-fit client. It's about a shared experience for both of you that needs far less explanation. Stories provide shortcuts that allow your best-fit clients to immediately see the connection and give you their attention. When someone sees a steak, no one has to explain to them that it's a kind of food. That's the kind of visceral connection that the right story makes with audiences.

- **Story Anchors**: Story anchors create an organization's "communication platform," the thematic core from which you develop specific marketing messages that bring your Capital S Story to life—and ultimately, fuel your brand.

- **Comprehensive**: The archetype and story anchors are foundational elements in an organization's business development and marketing. They guide messaging and tactics in all product and market segments. Why? Since archetypical stories transcend culture and time, they also transcend different market or product segments.

- **Collaborative**: In our experience, collaboration between those who develop your story and those who share it is essential to successfully applying the archetype, its companion story anchors, and to developing all marketing tools (website, sales materials, exhibition space, public relations or social media, etc.). Done well, the development of your authentic story becomes a team effort and is embraced across the organization.

HOW IT WORKS: THE WORDWRITE EXAMPLE

Now that we have our signposts mapped, let's talk about the real-world experience of uncovering, developing and sharing any organization's Capital S Story, including our own.

The example I'll share in this chapter is the work the WordWrite chefs did on our own company during our most recent trip to our test kitchen, in 2014.

The very first thing we need to do as we begin the StoryCrafting process with any organization is understand what they *think* the story is. This is the beginning of our Phase I, which we call StoryPlotting. In this initial exercise, there are two parts:

First, we ask a series of questions about the organization that we've come to call **The Five Burning Questions**. These questions may vary slightly from industry to industry or organization to organization. In the WordWrite example below, you'll see that they look like this.

1. **What is your organization's purpose?** (Author Simon Sinek calls this your "why.")
2. **What is the market demand for what you do?**
3. **What competitive position distinguishes you from your competitors?**
4. **What communication channels do you use to share your purpose and unique selling point or distinction to the audiences that you need to reach?**
5. **What is your call to action?** In other words, what would you like your audience to do once they see, hear or experience your story?

We'll get to WordWrite's answers in a minute. First, let's talk about why we ask these questions. In our experience, those inside an organization rarely agree on the answers! This is one of the reasons why so many classic marketing programs fail—if those in the organization can't agree on the organization's story, how are customers and potential customers supposed to understand it? When it's clear that there's no consensus on the answers, we push—really we do—in bringing this to our clients. Sometimes we lead them through the angst-filled step of creating consensus.

This process is critical. It's also not easy and on at least one occasion, our client decided to suspend the project because internally they simply could not come to agreement on, what are to us, the seminal building blocks of identifying a Capital S Story.

And this leads us to the second part of our initial exercise: A complete audit of all current or recent marketing materials and activities *and* a thorough secondary research review of all market research, intelligence and competitive analysis assistance from the organization's industry. We augment this research with informal, one-on-one or small group interviews with internal stakeholders.

We've learned that it's critical to understand what those *inside* the organization believe to be the successful elements of its story and to match that against what those *outside* the organization believe to be its story in the competitive marketplace of ideas.

We find that the elements of success that those inside an organization identify rarely match what we find from those outside the organization. That's why we invest a significant amount of time getting information about a client's story from both sources.

For example, we recently worked with a client whose executives agreed they were a "leading" firm in the industry. Yet when we analyzed secondary research, we discovered that of the "available" market share, the firm had less than 5 percent of the total. Can you be a "leading" firm and have less than a 5 percent market share? Probably not. But if you don't test your internal belief about your story in the marketplace of ideas, you may well be marketing your organization in a way that your audiences consider wholly irrelevant, or worse, inauthentic.

THESE PILLARS SUPPORT THE CAPITAL S STORY

The audit and research process help identify what we call an organization's **Story Fundamentals**. These are fact-based considerations that define the environment for the organization. An organization's Story Fundamentals are:

1. **Market Position:** It's not just the size of the market potential that matters, it's also where an organization stands within that market—this is critical to determining the appropriate storytelling tactics, technique and geographic reach.

2. **Competition:** We need to know the other players to determine an organization's unique value in ways that set it apart from competitors.

3. **Audiences:** An organization needs to know who they are trying to reach to properly frame language, story topics, how to prioritize the attributes of its products or services, and other message components. Often we ask, Who is your best-fit client?

4. **Segments:** Often, an organization's audience is really many smaller audiences. In such cases, it's very important to develop appropriate ways to share the same Capital S Story that speaks directly to each of these segments. For example, for a toolmaking company, two smaller audiences would be the people on the shop floor who use the tool, and the people in purchasing who buy the tool. The toolmaking company would need to share the same Capital S Story in ways that reach both segments. The story would be the same for both audiences. The difference is that it would be presented using pictures, words or experiences that each would understand best.

5. **Market Share:** An organization's position in the market is a critical determinant in how that organization can believably "carry" itself in terms of its story tone and content. What the audience expects to hear from an established market leader differs from what is expected of a start-up. As the organization engages its market, and its market position changes, so will its story and what its audiences expect to see, hear or experience when engaging with it.

OK, so let's take the **Five Burning Questions** and **Story Fundamentals** in turn. How did we apply them to WordWrite?

Here are the WordWrite answers to the **Five Burning Questions:**

1. **What is WordWrite's purpose as we see it?**
   We are on a mission to remake marketing by focusing on what works, the ageless power of story.

2. **What is the need for what we do?**
   Research and experience both prove that classic advertising, marketing and public relations fail to consistently deliver measurable results.

3. **In our opinion, what distinguishes WordWrite from its competitors?**
   (From interviews with WordWrite staff):

   - WordWrite does things different. It is a contrarian.
   - Story is what makes WordWrite different.

4. **What is the best way to communicate WordWrite's purpose and unique selling point or distinction to the audiences that we need to reach?**
   As an agency that began in PR and is expanding into social media and digital marketing, our best tools are those that we employ on behalf of our clients, from PR to digital marketing. We must be the *chef who eats his own cooking* if we are to demonstrate to clients that what we do will work for them.

5. **What is our call to action? What would we like our audience to do once they see, hear or experience our story?**
   As storytellers committed to great storytelling, we want our audiences to engage with our Story, and if it's appropriate, we want them to begin a dialogue that

leads to a long-term relationship as clients, partners, employees and supporters.

And here are WordWrite's **Story Fundamentals**:

1. **Market Position:** We are among the top 100 independent firms in the country, based upon two trade publication rankings.
2. **Competition:** We are ranked in the top 10 of firms in our home city, based upon a decade of client and competitive data that we have compiled internally. We compete consistently with two to three agencies that focus on business-to-business opportunities in our home city.
3. **Audiences:** Because we focus on business-to-business clients, we typically speak to vice presidents or directors of communications or marketing as well as to the "C-Suite," usually CEOs.
4. **Segments:** Based upon our historic client mix, we are a nationally ranked firm serving health care, manufacturing, professional services and technology clients.
5. **Market Share:** Based upon annual sales reported to the local business journal by the top 25 firms in our home region, we have about 5 percent market share.

Once we had answers to WordWrite's Five Burning Questions and a good understanding of our Story Fundamentals, we could move on to the process of identifying story archetypes and then story anchors that would bring the WordWrite Capital S Story to life. Remember, the goal here is to align our story with our mission in a way that it requires as little explanation as possible—we want it to be seamless.

Using the wheel of 12 archetypes we explored in the previous chapter, the WordWrite team gathered the raw material we had so far and identified three potential archetypes that aligned with our story and mission:

- **Explorer:** Because we seek to remake our industry and chart a new path
- **Outlaw:** Because we fight the conventional wisdom that defines classic marketing
- **Champion (a mash-up of caregiver and creator from below):** Because we employ storytelling to make our clients the heroes in their own stories.

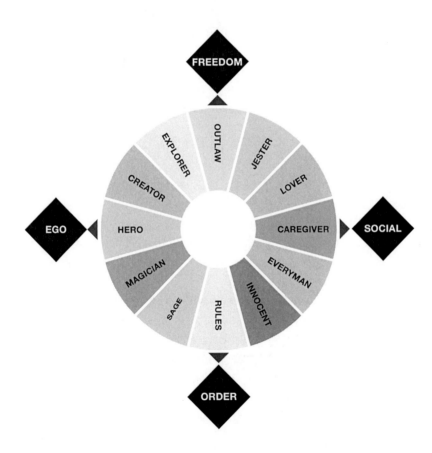

To help us determine which of these potential archetypes best fit WordWrite, we reviewed the results of our internal interviews and organized them according to our interpretation of each archetype:

WordWrite as Explorer:

- *Where others are content, explorers are driven to learn.*
- *Explorers provide an evolutionary and competitive advantage.*
- *Explorers have the intangible desire to explore and challenge the boundaries of what we know, in turn providing benefits to society.*

And so, WordWrite is an EXPLORER because it is evolving from a traditional public relations firm to a strategic communications consultancy driven by story.

- WordWrite's goal is to remake the public relations industry.
- WordWrite is breaking new ground.
- It is in our nature to question, learn and understand.
- A change to the new and unfamiliar is often met with skepticism and resistance.
- WordWrite is innovating; the majority of potential clients are not early adopters.

WordWrite as Outlaw:

- *Outlaws decide to live outside the law rather than submitting to rules.*
- *Outlaw heroes (e.g., Robin Hood) can arise because people are opposed to the sometimes brutal nature of common law.*
- *Outlaw: one that is unconventional or rebellious.*

WordWrite is an OUTLAW because it does things differently.

- WordWrite takes a contrary position or attitude about how public relations is practiced.
- WordWrite is the anti-agency agency.
- WordWrite has a big, hairy audacious goal (BHAG): to possess the most valued PR model in the world.
- WordWrite is remaking the PR industry, changing the paradigm.
- WordWrite has a completely open culture.
- WordWriters can literally do anything they want that will foster their professional development and enable the business to pursue its big ideas.

WordWrite as Champion:

- *A champion is not afraid to lose.*
- *Champions always compete with purpose and passion.*
- *A champion focuses on continuous daily improvement.*

WordWrite is a CHAMPION because Story is what makes us different.

- Storytelling has moved mankind for thousands of years.
- WordWrite has spent years honing StoryCrafting[SM], its proprietary process for helping organizations develop a well-told story that connects it to its audiences.
- In a complex, hyper-digitized, business-to-business world, story is the most compelling and effective competitive strategy available to deliver persuasive communications.

After lots of discussion, our team settled on the Explorer archetype as the one that best defines who we are as a company, and who we seek to be in our marketplace for all of our audiences.

As I wrote earlier, an archetype by itself does not a story make. If you visit the WordWrite website, you're not going to find the word EXPLORER plastered all over everything. That's not how great storytelling works. It is both more strategic and more subtle than that.

The strategy and the subtlety are delivered through what we call **Story Anchors**. Frequently, story anchors leverage modern-day examples of archetypes to bring the story to life.

Here are examples of the story anchors we considered to share the WordWrite story:

Example #1

Ever held a business meeting at Starbucks? Just as Starbucks has reinvented the way the public views coffee shops as more than a place to have coffee—at WordWrite we are reinventing the public relations industry to center on authentic stories as a way to build brand rather than traditional marketing tactics.

Example #2

If you are familiar with the early days of Apple when Steve Jobs and Steve Wozniak had a vision to transform the way we viewed and used computers and phones, you might consider us in a similar vein. At WordWrite, we see the basic principles of public relations as outdated. Things are different today and we believe in changing the industry to better meet the needs of businesses and the way people consume and recall information using storytelling.

The collaborative process of evaluating story anchors such as these led WordWrite to an ultimate formulation. Here are a few examples of how we've imbedded our archetype and our story anchors into everything we do:

From the home page of our website after we completed the exercise and updated the website in 2020:

READY TO BE THE HERO OF YOUR OWN STORY?

We will help you uncover your great, untold story.

To the description of our firm that we put at the end of every article, blog or press release we write about ourselves:

About WordWrite:

WordWrite is an award-winning strategic public relations, digital and inbound marketing agency. The Pittsburgh-based agency helps companies uncover, develop and share their Capital S Story, the most important marketing tool companies have, to reveal why someone would do business with them, partner with them or work for them. For more than 18 years, WordWrite has advised health care, manufacturing, nonprofit and professional services businesses, including Fortune 100 companies, with services from crisis communications to product launches.

As you can see, the word EXPLORER doesn't appear in our marketing. It's in there, though, infused and understood just as a diner—even one who doesn't like red meat—understands that a steak is something you eat.

SHARING YOUR STORY: AS VITAL AS KNOWING IT

Once an organization's Capital S Story is uncovered and developed, there are a few more steps to take so that the organization can share that story effectively. Remember that in an earlier chapter, we identified the three aspects of a great Capital S Story:

- Rooted in fact (authentic)
- Shared by fluent storytellers
- A commitment to continually read the audience to ensure that engagement is happening

So once you've uncovered and developed your authentic Capital S Story, you must select those best able to share it, and ensure that as you share it, you're engaging the audiences you most want to reach in an ongoing conversation that drives business results. Let's look at these two aspects of your Capital S Story.

YOUR ORGANIZATION'S FLUENT STORYTELLERS

Once an organization's story is expanded, based upon the best archetype, that organization must determine the storytelling roles of its leaders—identifying those who are best suited to tell the organization's story. For example, remember that in our first chapter, we met fluent storytellers from Nike, Southwest and Blendtec.

Our point then (and now) is that your story is best told by a small group of leaders who are passionate about and best represent the story. At this point, it's time to step out of the test kitchen and into the real world.

As a storyteller my entire career, it's no surprise that I fulfill these roles authentically and often at WordWrite. But you're not going to learn much about cooking at home by religiously following the professional chef around the cutting board. So let's put the WordWrite example aside to focus on what we've seen in other organizations.

Let's start with a point I made earlier: Too many organizations stick with a founder, inventor or CEO or other storyteller just because they think that's who should be sharing the story. They look at the organization chart, or who's in charge, and without considering other factors, pick the top dog.

That's shortsighted. If your story is authentic, and the storyteller is as well, then it's important to have your best storyteller out front sharing the story. And that may well not be the CEO or leader. It could be an employee who best represents the organization's story.

The person who best represents the story is the person who is living it. It could be a doctor in a health care system, or a nurse, it could be a firefighter rather than the fire chief. It needs to be someone who is a good communicator, not just someone who is in the right place on the organizational chart.

At WordWrite for example, I may have storyteller in my title, but I am hardly the only storyteller. All of our vice presidents, account supervisors and team members have expertise that, given the situation, makes them the right person to be sharing an aspect of our story. For example, I'm somewhat active on Instagram and other social media platforms, but when we need to demonstrate our expertise in this area, other team members are the right choice to be sharing that aspect of our story. The Capital S Story is a strategic endeavor. Sharing it via the appropriate means—social media, print, video, etc.—still requires team members who have superior understanding of the right tools and how to bring the Capital S Story to life by using those tools.

Again, this is where true storytelling success involves strategy and subtlety to drive real results.

Let's take just one example of what *not to do* in picking your storyteller. One is painful enough, trust me.

When legendary Microsoft founder Bill Gates decided to relinquish the CEO role at the company, he (and apparently everyone else at Microsoft), looked at the org chart and picked the next in line: Steve Ballmer, who had previously led Microsoft's sales. A dutiful soldier and leader, and certainly accomplished, Ballmer was not only given control of the company, he also inherited the chief storyteller role previously held by Gates.

Gates, a quiet, thin, cerebral visionary whose trademark glasses frame his introspective face, was famous not only for leading Microsoft but also for his far-reaching thinking, often expressed in lengthy memos he wrote to senior Microsoft leaders. Often, they were leaked outside the company and read by industry leaders and journalists for hints of the technology future.

Ballmer, on the other hand, was a tall, enthusiastic bald guy who'd spent most of his career as many sales leaders do, whipping up the troops to drive sales.

The contrast was painful. Ballmer may have been a great company leader (though *Fast Company* called him "A salesman without product vision" in a much-referenced and unflattering assessment of his term as CEO).

Even if Ballmer was a great CEO, he was decidedly not a fluent storyteller for the company. The contrast between his style and that of Gates was not only dramatic, it was off-putting. YouTube is filled with compendiums of his worst moments as chief storyteller during his CEO tenure.

Perhaps the worst was his speech to a group of developers in which Ballmer was his usual enthusiastic self, bouncing around the stage, pounding his fists, extolling the audience (of developers) to stand and cheer like the Microsoft sales force, as beads of sweat glistened on his forehead and the sweat stains on his blue shirt soaked not only his armpits and his chest but also all the way through his shirt collar.

Microsoft is still a very large and successful company. After four years, though, Ballmer retired. Please don't repeat the Ballmer lesson in your company. You probably don't have billions of dollars in the bank, as Microsoft does, so you can't afford this kind of experiment. Pick the right storyteller to tell your authentic story.

READING THE AUDIENCE

Our final step in Phase I of StoryCrafting determines the most appropriate strategies to "read the audience" and assure that the sharing of the organization's story is effectively measured through interaction with the audiences the organization seeks to engage. You must conceptually define the type of performance measures and "standards of success" that are relevant to marketing activities for your organization.

By tapping the reservoirs of powerful stories from history, popular culture and modern business success, you can adapt a powerful story archetype and create a custom narrative that aligns with your organization's authentic story and meshes with your daily business reality.

This detailed, integrated story narrative, like the draft for a great play or film, or the outline of a great book, is the map that guides your organization in sharing your great story to deliver results.

Our collaboration in the StoryPlotting phase is distilled in an outline with recommendations on how to develop a comprehensive plan to share the organization's story, including where and when to tell it, along with the tools and techniques to accurately measure the engagement of the organization's targeted audiences and thus, its results.

One of the most consistent criticisms of marketing (see our chapter on John Wanamaker) is that the discipline is one of those touchy-feely, "I can't tell what's working" endeavors. Nothing could be further from the truth. And if you want to ensure that you reap the most success from sharing your authentic story, then you *must* measure how it's playing in the marketplace of ideas.

Let me show you how we do that at WordWrite. The example below is from a recent client. We believe you shouldn't spend *a single dollar* on your marketing unless you can tell whether that dollar is doing anything for you. And it's no different if you're sharing the best marketing asset you have, your great untold story.

Our measurement approach is adapted from the great work done by one of the true visionaries in marketing measurement, Katie Delahaye Paine. She identified three kinds of measurement for success: Outputs, Outtakes and Outcomes. In the example below, you'll see how we have adapted her work so that this system of measurement aligns with sharing your great, untold story.

Metrics are developed jointly with CLIENT leadership at the outset of our engagement. We typically divide them into these three categories:

Outputs: Timely and cost-effective execution of public relations activities on behalf of CLIENT on a consistent basis;

Outtakes: Broad, accurate and compelling articulation of the CLIENT story, as evidenced by feedback from internal and external stakeholders, target audiences, media coverage and visibility of the CLIENT in the news media (measured quarterly); and

Outcomes: Increased activity, in terms of media, website traffic, potential prospects and leads who reach out to the CLIENT (measured quarterly).

Examples of each include the following:

Category*	Activity
Outputs	Article creation and/or distribution, press release creation and/or distribution, media outreach to reporters
Outtakes	Number of page views on website, number of materials downloaded, number of website visitors, improved ratio of website referral traffic vs. organic source traffic, number of agreed upon key messages articulated in an article or news story
Outcomes	Increase in number of calls or emails to CLIENT inquiring about partnership, participation, sponsorships, etc. directly related to/resulting from outputs mentioned above, as well as attraction of additional website traffic to key areas of focus

Accurate measurement of the above categories requires a collaborative collection of data from both the client and agency team.

If you don't know if your story is connecting with those you most want to reach—your best-fit clients—then you are no better off than the condition attributed to John Wanamaker a century ago, "Half the money I spend on advertising is wasted; the trouble is I don't know which half."

With your authentic story, your fluent storytellers *and* a commitment to ensure that you're reaching and engaging your audiences, you'll make John Wanamaker proud by proving that old quote to be nothing more than a historical footnote in the annals of successful marketing.

THE GREATEST STORY EVER SHARED—YOURS

A great story is only great once it is shared. So it is with your organization's story. Phase II of a WordWrite StoryCrafting engagement, which we have dubbed StorySharing, is focused on bringing a client's Capital S Story to life by sharing it with everyone who needs to hear it.

When, where and how a client's story is shared is determined by the work we've done together in the first phase. Too many marketing or public relations campaigns begin at the level of tactical execution—how many press releases, what kind of events, etc., without first determining the story to be shared.

This is the fundamental difference in our approach to story-telling that enables our clients to enjoy better results—decisions on how to allocate resources are made only AFTER determining the story and confirming how its results will be measured. Without determining the plot of the story, the roles that will bring the story alive, and the look and feel of the story's happy ending, how can an organization ensure that it enjoys the results that it seeks from its story?

Once you've developed your Capital S Story, then every strategy, tactic and activity selected should further the story. And every strategy, tactic and activity should be continually measured to ensure that results are delivered.

As in a great stage performance, you must "read the audience" again and again to ensure that your story is engaging those you want to reach.

In our work for our own firm, we consistently measure engagement with our social media and website and we track a variety of metrics every week. If we see that the level of engagement is slipping, we analyze and adjust—we are always looking to keep our audience engaged so that we can deliver success for ourselves as well as our clients.

Let me share an example for a large health care client. These illustrations demonstrate the story and how we measured (and delivered) success by applying our StoryCrafting principles.

AREA OF FOCUS

FOCUS AREAS	GOALS
Consumer health article placement and strategic/timely pitches:	Complement and Enhance Center Openings
Seasonal ■ Allergies, flu, youth wellness ■ Sun safety, cold weather care, packing for vacation	Position our physicians and health staff as experts in non-emergent care and seasonal conditions
Illness and Injury ■ Pneumonia, bronchitis, colds ■ Breaks, sprains, cuts, safety precautions	Achieve more media hits in more markets by engaging news media more frequently
Industry Educational ■ UC vs ER ■ Access, cost ■ Understanding health care options	

First, we established goals (in this case, positioning our client as go-to experts, most closely aligned with the sage or navigator archetype) and then from that, we identified topical health care issues where the client's expertise could be employed to share its story (see chart above).

As you can see in the chart below, we closely measured our success in activity (outputs) and how well the marketplace of ideas, in this case, journalists, was receptive to the story (outtakes).

Q2 OUTPUTS AND OUTTAKES

Pitched at least one topic every week to journalists in 16 states
Including mommy bloggers and national publications

OUTPUTS	OUTTAKES

Planned topics:
• Spring allergies
• Spring cleaning your medicine cabinet
• Hay fever
• Ticks & Lyme disease
• Infected cuts and scrapes
• Stress fractures
• Dehydration
	• 11 pitches received interest
	  □ Wrote 13 (not including HAROs)
	
	• 4 bylines published
	  □ Wrote 5
	
	• 4 interviews arranged

Pre-opening outreach: • Understanding your healthcare options: ER or UC • Center openings	• 9 HAROs submitted • 2 profiles published (Nurses Week)
EHS topics • Heat-related illnesses • Ticks & Lyme disease • Employee wellness	• 3 news releases distributed • 3 media alerts distributed
24 Identified opportunities: • Skincare, sun protection, sunscreen, dehydration, ticks and Lyme disease, gypsy moth caterpillars, back-to-school health, ERs in Florida	

Q2 OUTCOMES SNAPSHOT

16 MEDIA HITS
8 MARKETS

FROM FIRST QUARTER
13 media hits
11 markets

- **"Gypsy Moths Back in Season"**
  -WOLF-TV Fox 56 (Wilkes-Barre, PA)

- **"Scientists predict a surge in ticks this spring due to warm winter"**
  - WHSV ABC 3)Harrisonburg, VA)

- **"Allergy Season Tips"**
  - WBOY NBC 12 (Morgantown, WV)

- **"Going to the ER or Urgent Care Center? How to make the right choice"**
  - Naples Daily News (Naples, FL)

- **"Why Employers Should Take Lyme Diesease More Seriously"**
  - HR.com (National)

- **"Facts About Sunscreen and Sun Protection"**
  - Live Science (National)

- **"National Nurses Week Profile"**
  - Western PA Healthcare News (Pittsburgh, PA)

- **"Here's How Dehydration Can Sneak Up On You"**
  - Huffington Post (National)

24 PROACTIVE
MEDIA OPPORTUNITIES

13 OPPORTUNITIES IN Q1

13 CONSUMER & EHS TOPICS
PITCHED

13 TOPICS IN Q1

16 STATES
WE PITCHED TO

NEARLY 80 MARKETS

As with any marketing endeavor, the proof is in the results. The chart above shows how well we did in sharing the story (outputs), gaining adoption of the client's story in media interest (outtakes) and then finally, actual coverage (outcomes).

This is just one example. Your story is unique, and so will be your application of reading the audience. One commonality should be a solid application of measurement principles, such as outputs, outtakes and outcomes.

By constructing an effective story, sharing it most appropriately, and asking the audience for feedback, you will ensure that your organization enjoys a true dialogue with those you want to reach.

For your organization, the greatest story ever told is your own—the unique, authentic and compelling narrative that defines your reasons for communicating with the audiences you seek to engage. Whether your purpose is to sell, influence or educate, in the 21st century, only the ageless power of a story well told can break through the clutter of information overload.

There's one caution as you start applying these principles in your organization: Companies that sell to other companies and those that sell consumer goods and services often have vastly different stories to share. We'll explain why in the next chapter.

StoryCrafter's Toolkit
Chapter 6

If you're reading the printed edition of the book, access these links and resources through your web browser at: www.capitalsstory.com/storycrafterstoolkit.

If you're reading an electronic edition, just click the links in this box to access all the resources.

- A goldfish has a longer attention span than you
- Simon Sinek: Start with Why TEDx talk
- Alan Alda, fluent storyteller for science
- Joseph Campbell on Carl Jung and archetypes
- Steve Ballmer on his Microsoft journey

IF YOU'RE SELLING TO B2B OR B2C, DO YOU SHARE YOUR STORY DIFFERENTLY?

Walk the toothpaste aisle of any large grocery store and you'll be confronted by a confusing reality: Thousands and thousands of boxes of toothpaste, hundreds and hundreds of color combinations, untold sales slogans and yet, a small voice in your brain, struggling with sensory overload, crying out: *"Aren't most of these toothpastes pretty much the same?"*

In a word: Yes!

Welcome to the stupefying and paralyzing conundrum facing most consumer brands seeking to share their story.

On the one hand, toothpaste is toothpaste. It is the classic consumer commodity—aside from all those colors and sales slogans and tweaks to basic ingredients, it's hard to differentiate one brand from another. After all, aren't they all dentist-recommended? Yes, because why would ANY dentist recommend that you NOT brush your teeth?

Several decades of marketing effort have tried to create some identifiable differentiation for toothpaste and similar consumer products and yet consumer research shows time and again that consumers can identify and remember far fewer brands, flavors, colors, etc. of toothpaste than are sold.

Which leads me to this thought: If your product is truly a commodity indistinguishable from its competitors, isn't that possibly the best reason why you need to share your authentic story? (Yes, it is, and we'll come back to that later).

For most of us, the business stories we know best are undoubtedly those of organizations selling consumer products. It's only natural since the global economy is about 70 percent composed of businesses selling products and services to consumers (B2C), and only 30 percent composed of businesses selling products or services to another business (B2B).

So the business stories with which you are most familiar are attached to the most basic, indistinguishable consumer products. This realization has multiple implications for you and your organization when seeking to share your great, untold story. To be successful in developing and sharing your own story, you need to understand the following three things:

- First, the kind of story you share to drive B2C sales is going to be very different than the story you share to drive B2B sales.
- Second, the stories we know best—which are often attached to some of the biggest consumer brands in the world—may be poor models for your organization, whether you are selling to consumers or other businesses. That's because uncovering, developing and sharing your company's story is not about repeating a well-known consumer story; it's about developing your own Capital S Story.
- And third, to have success, many consumer brands don't seem to have much of a story at all, which could confuse you about the value of your story. Think about it: Proctor and Gamble's first brand was a soap. How many soap brands does the company have today, and how strong do those individual stories need to be if the consumer knows they are coming from P&G? P&G spends more than just about any other consumer goods company (and they employ storytelling at many levels). Yet for many of its brands, it's just sell and sell some more—and often what they're selling are basic

commodities that have little if any story to support them. They are missing an opportunity. These consumer brands often rely on cute marketing tricks, backed by enormous budgets for advertising. This can work to sell basic products if there's really not much of a story, or the decision is driven primarily by price. And yet, couldn't you tell the story behind Crest or Colgate, both of which have a long-standing presence in the marketplace? Yes—and they would do better if they had a story to share. In my mind, they exist in the marketplace but not at the level that they could. They're missing opportunity.

In this chapter, we'll explore these differences and explain how you can effectively share your authentic business story with your best-fit clients, based upon whether you sell to consumers or other businesses.

As we learned in previous chapters, for your organization, the greatest story ever told is your own—the unique, authentic and compelling narrative that defines your reasons for communicating with the audiences you seek to engage.

What's the best way to make this work for you and your organization? Let's take a look.

THE CONSUMER STORYTELLING CONUNDRUM

The bulk of products and services in this world are sold to consumers. And the majority of these sales are typically of low-cost items. Think of the world around us: from bedsheets to undergarments, toothbrushes to copy paper, most of these consumer items entail very little easily discernable differentiation.

When it comes to jump drives, for example, what are the true differences from one brand to another? Sure, they come in colors and sizes, but … they all do the same thing, right?

And what about consumer services? Consider drycleaners for instance. While factors such as convenience, quality of service or price factor into the equation, how often do we make decisions about this sort of service based upon the story behind the service?

Unless you bring to life the story behind the "commoditized" consumer product or service you provide, you leave your company to decisions made based upon boring table stakes such as mere competence, location or price. Is that enough for your great marketing differentiator?

Obviously, my answer is no. Developing the story behind your story is the true secret sauce to power your business to new heights.

If you're open to developing the story behind the story of your consumer-focused company, we first have to return to the toothpaste aisle to understand the two essential motivations for true B2C storytelling. The first essential motivation is that you want to stand out from everybody else, right?

The second essential motivation is eradicating the brain confusion that comes from too many choices for what is basically the same product. That sensory overload you're experiencing comes from a biological issue that psychologist Barry Schwartz described in his 2004 book, *The Paradox of Choice—Why More Is Less.*

In his work, Schwartz demonstrates that the human brain works best when it has a small set of choices to decide. When the number of choices far exceeds the brain's ability to decide, paralysis sets in and decision making becomes difficult.

Schwartz argues that the global consumer economy, driven by the engine of American commerce, has turned into a circus of sensory overload in which success and freedom are measured by the degree of individual freedom and self-determination a consumer possesses to make purchase decisions. In other words, in our modern consumer world, more is better.

Schwartz believes all this choice is detrimental to our psychological and emotional well-being. In his work, he argues that the existence of so many choices has become a problem instead of an advantage.

The psychologist goes on to make larger claims about too many choices making us less happy and to suggest other theories that aren't relevant to our understanding of storytelling. For our purposes, let's focus on that confusion in the toothpaste aisle.

How can we make our sales of consumer goods and services distinctive when we sell in a category that provides too many choices for our best-fit clients to make a good decision?

How about by providing a "story behind the story" that gives context to what might seem to some as commoditized products or services? In other words, if I can have my carpets cleaned by three companies, and the prices are about the same, what else can I evaluate to make the best decision? How about the story behind the company providing the service? Who are these people? Why should I buy from them, as opposed to their competitors?

See the sidebar on Tom's of Maine and TOMS for two excellent, well-known (and financially successful) examples of powerful "story behind the story" B2C storytelling.

Tom's of Maine is the family-founded, back-to-nature company best known for its all-natural toothpaste, one of the first on the market and definitely the one with the best brand recognition. The company originally challenged the conventional wisdom of the 1970s by taking on the mass-produced approach to toothpaste by creating a line made solely from natural ingredients. Since then, the company's expanded far beyond toothpaste, all the while keeping to its Capital S Story roots.

TOMS, first known as TOMS Shoes, is a distinct company that focuses on social justice much in the same way that Tom's of Maine focuses on environmental purity. From its initial shoe-based product line, which promised one pair of shoes for a shoeless child in a developing country for every pair bought by a modern consumer, TOMS has also extended its Capital S Story far beyond the original product line that made it successful.

What the Tom's/TOMS stories illustrate for us is that a good story behind the story—even for consumer brands in a product category that's stupendously overcrowded—eliminates the problem of too many choices. It gives consumers a reason to select one brand over another.

Or as TOMS' founder Blake Mycoskie once put it, "Having a story is what separates us. People don't just wear our shoes, they tell our story."

THE DEEP ARC OF B2B STORYTELLING

What if what you sell is far more complex than toothpaste? And what if you're selling to a large and skeptical corporate purchasing committee rather than someone desperate to whiten his or her teeth?

While the challenge for B2C companies is to identify the "story behind the story" for what are often numbingly indistinctive products or services, the challenge for many B2B companies is to create differentiation by peeling back complexity in products and services.

For these companies, great storytelling can help turn complexity into clarity and create a memorable narrative that provides the differentiation they need to succeed. Let's look at an example.

A few years ago, our firm worked for a brief time with a company that made "fake" nuclear medicine equipment. The entire premise seems expensively ludicrous at first—what hospital or medical provider wants to purchase fully functional but fully useless equipment?

The reason becomes much clearer when we ask a few questions that can be answered through a strong narrative story.

What are some of the greatest issues for hospitals and medical providers entrusted with employing unstable radioactive materials to conduct diagnostic tests or nuclear medicine treatments? Well, how about accidents that sicken workers or patients? Or perhaps improper handling of unstable radioactive materials that causes other problems? These are just two potentially bad outcomes of poorly trained staff working with dangerous radioactive materials.

So how should a hospital or other medical provider train staff to properly handle unstable radioactive materials to ensure patient and worker safety?

What if they could practice on equipment *exactly like the equipment they will use with patients* and experience all sorts of potential accident or mishap scenarios and learn how to prevent them without the danger of handling "real" radioactive materials or endangering workers or patients?

Now you can see the benefit of our example company's work. Yet the way they were sharing this story was hardly compelling, and the staff was struggling to make headway with potential clients. This is the classic B2B storytelling scenario. In this sort of situation, it's useful to think of the example company's story much like a book that unfolds in chapters. If we were to outline this story, the chapters would flow like this:

Chapter 1   The biggest problem in nuclear medicine: accidents with radioactive materials

Chapter 2   Face it, there's no easy way to train staff to prevent this problem

Chapter 3   Wait! What if there *were* a new kind of solution to train staff to prevent nuclear medicine accidents?

Chapter 4   Our company makes a line of fully functional, fully safe nuclear medicine equipment

Chapter 5   Here's a case study of how one medical provider reduced nuclear medicine accidents by training with our equipment

And etc.

So this is the B2B corollary of *The Paradox of Choice*. It's not that there are too many choices when selling your product or service; it's that fully understanding what you have to offer may require breaking a complex idea into a story format so that it can more easily be understood—and remembered.

In addition, there is a difference when selling B2B products versus services. Let's understand why by first understanding B2B prospects.

For decades, publications ranging from *BusinessWeek* to *Inc.* and even *The Huffington Post* have bemoaned the fact that so many business leaders were merely "C" students, or to put it more charitably, passably good at every subject and not great at any one subject. In other words, leaders in the C-Suite are typically good generalists, but we shouldn't expect them to be deeply knowledgeable in any one area.

This dynamic creates two kinds of considerations for B2B sales, depending upon whether you are selling products or services. Let's look at products first.

Because of the credentials of those who typically occupy the C-Suite, to succeed in selling complex B2B *products*, you must share the value of what you do (your story) in a way that doesn't require an advanced degree to understand it.

Time and again, one of the mistakes we see with potential client companies is a focus on selling to the experts rather than the decision makers. For example, technology companies frequently focus on marketing to the technical experts in their prospect companies. Almost without exception, these individuals may understand the technology but they DO NOT sign the checks to buy anything. It's the C-Suite occupants that need to understand the need for the IT product—the CEO or CFO who is NOT an IT expert. To effectively sell products to those who sign the checks, you need a story that makes the complex understandable.

When it comes to selling B2B *services*, we see a different dynamic that requires storytelling focused on who's delivering the services, not what kind of services are offered.

We've worked with many professional service firms, from accountants to engineers to lawyers, and these folks can get terribly lost in focusing on the certifications and letters behind the names of the principals *at the expense of revealing who these people are and why they should be trusted with the client's most precious business issues.*

Countless surveys over the last several decades have shown that among the top five most trusted outside advisors to business leaders are professionals, especially accountants and lawyers. Yet time and again, we find that professional service firms fail to share the story of *the people who want to be the client's trusted advisers.*

Businesses hire an accounting firm to keep them out of financial trouble; they hire a law practice to keep them out of legal trouble. Yet too many accountants and lawyers want to market by selling their formal qualifications instead of the story behind the individuals who will ensure that their clients stay out of financial or legal trouble.

Years ago, we worked with a mid-sized actuarial and employee benefits firm that was competing against some of the biggest names in the business. The skill level of the people carefully managing the assets and interests of the firm's clients was a key differentiator in the marketplace. Yet the focus was on the darned certifications and letters, not the people. When we began focusing on the people, amazing things happened.

We shared the story of how one principal's history with motorcycles made a difference in his approach to risk; for another, we highlighted his military service as the Air Force guy inside the missile silo with his finger on the red button to tell the story of why clients should trust him with their assets.

Trust me, actuaries are not usually known for their effusive, emotional behavior. So imagine the satisfaction—for them, their firm and for us—when prospects and clients remembered these stories and began asking to work with these individuals *because of their personal stories.* We saw smiling actuaries, people who went out of their way to thank us for helping them to connect their personal, passionate narratives *with what they did for their clients.*

NOT ALL EFFECTIVE STORIES ARE THE SAME

As we've learned in this chapter, everything we now know about effective storytelling to attract best-fit clients has to be filtered through an important lens: Are you selling to consumers, or to other businesses?

And once you understand that B2C and B2B stories are different, you must approach the process and the audience for your great, untold story with different considerations in mind.

For B2C sales, the challenge is rising above what are often indistinguishable products and services to focus on "the story behind the story" of what your company does.

For B2B sales, the challenge is first to understand that selling products or services requires a slightly different focus in terms of how you construct your story.

If you're selling B2B products, the likely complexity of what you sell creates the necessity to break the value of your products into a more understandable story that your best-fit clients can more readily comprehend—and respond to with interest and enthusiasm.

And if you're selling B2B services, the focus has to be on the story of those delivering the services, not on the services themselves.

At this juncture, we've covered nearly all the basics of uncovering, developing and sharing your organization's great, untold story. We have a few more stops to make before you can begin the journey to share your organization's story most effectively.

We'll take a look at one of the biggest storytelling roadblocks—which is really one of your greatest opportunities—in our next chapter, storytelling in social media.

Successful B2C storytelling: A tale of two Toms

Earlier in this chapter, we reviewed the challenges in selling highly commoditized consumer products by sharing an authentic business story. Two great illustrations of overcoming this challenge from two Toms: Tom's of Maine, and TOMS Shoes.

Tom's of Maine, founded in 1970 by husband and wife Tom and Kate Chappell, challenged the conventional wisdom at the time by taking the mass-produced notion of toothpaste and returning this basic product to its roots with a line made solely from natural ingredients.

As the company's website describes it, the couple "moved to Maine from Philadelphia in 1968, looking for a healthier, simpler life for their growing family. They discovered the benefits of natural and unprocessed food, and started looking for the same qualities in personal care products. But all they found were labels listing artificial flavors, fragrances, sweeteners, colors and preservatives. So they decided to create their own."

From its Kennebunkport roots, the small company was quickly associated with the back-to-nature storyline of many natural consumer products that were coming to market in the early 1970s. Remember, this was the same era when the federal government created the Environmental Protection Agency, and environmental disasters (including Love Canal, an entire neighborhood abandoned because of toxic waste buried beneath it) were hot topics nationally. Consumers concerned about environmental evils loved the Tom's story, and the company grew quickly. Today, it produces 90 oral- and body-care products, which are sold at more than 40,000 retail outlets worldwide.

And while Tom's is perhaps best known for its toothpaste, the company lived its authentic story from the beginning with its very first product, Clearlake Laundry Detergent, which the company describes as "the nation's first liquid, non-phosphate laundry detergent." From that beginning in 1970, part of the company's authentic, natural ingredient story has evolved into an ongoing environmental commitment that includes publishing the company's sustainability progress and goals in what it calls an annual Goodness Report.

Today, Tom's products include soaps, toothpastes, deodorants and mouthwashes. Tom's fluoride toothpastes are the only natural alternatives to common, industrial-ingredient dentifrices to earn the American Dental Association's Seal of Acceptance.

Like many great small enterprises with authentic stories, Tom's became very attractive to more conventional, larger companies. In 2006, Colgate-Palmolive, one of the largest makers of "traditional" toothpastes, bought a controlling interest in Tom's of Maine for $100 million. True to its founding principles (and thus its authentic story), the purchase agreement included stipulations that the policies and company culture of Tom's be retained.

While TOMS (originally TOMS Shoes) is sometimes confused with Tom's of Maine, it is a distinct entity. If Tom's of Maine is New England purity, TOMS Shoes is California celebrity activism. The only similarity is a tremendously authentic story.

TOMS, based in Playa del Ray, California, began much later than Tom's of Maine (2002) and its authentic story builds on consumer storytelling principles that the older Tom's pioneered.

Founded by Blake Mycoskie, a former participant in the TV reality series, *The Amazing Race,* TOMS shoes are designed to rise above the same-old sameness that sometimes pervades consumer goods. Mycoskie, who first visited Argentina while competing on the reality TV show, was initially inspired to create and sell shoes based on the Argentine alpargata design, a kind of slip-on shoe worn by average Argentines.

While the shoes themselves were a distinct story, it was the larger story behind TOMS that propelled the company's success. As Mycoskie tells it, he returned to Argentina on vacation in 2006, and saw local polo players wearing alpargatas. While doing volunteer work in the outskirts of Buenos Aires, Mycoskie noticed many of the children were running the streets barefoot.

So when he developed an alpargata variation for the North American market, Mycoskie decided to provide a free pair of shoes to youth in Argentina and other developing nations for every pair he sold.

This is the essence of the larger "story behind the story" of TOMS and it extends to the company name, which is a variation on the word "tomorrow" taken from the original concept, "Shoes for Tomorrow Project." The TOMS story was compelling from the start: Following a *Los Angeles Times* article early in the company's history, orders flooded in for nine times the available stock; 10,000 pairs were sold in the first year.

The company has continued to evolve its larger story behind the story: Its annual "One Day Without Shoes" event involves participants forgoing shoes for one day to raise awareness about the impact shoes can have on a child's life.

The event has had corporate sponsors including AOL, Flickr and the Discovery Channel.

In more recent years, the "story behind the story" of TOMS has led to creation of consumer goods including eyewear, with a similar goal of providing eyeglasses to those who can't afford them. More recently, they created TOMS Roasting, a coffee company that helps poor communities around the world by enabling safe drinking water projects.

The TOMS business model has been copied by many other retailers. It's known as the "one for all" model, because of the commitment to equate the purchase of one consumer good with one donated to those who can't afford it. Today, brands from Bombas socks to Warby Parker eyewear have adopted this model in hopes of creating their own larger story for what are often indistinguishable consumer goods.

Author Daniel H. Pink has said this business model is "expressly built for purpose maximization," meaning TOMS is selling both products and its ideal. Another phrase used to describe the business model has been "caring capitalism." While both of these descriptions may be accurate, for our purposes, that "purpose maximization" or "caring capitalism" is another way of saying there's a bigger "story behind the story" that defines TOMS and these copycat brands.

It's probably unsurprising that, as with Tom's of Maine, this valuable "story behind the story" led to a 50 percent sale of TOMS to Bain Capital. Reuters valued the 2014 transaction at $625 million.

In a parallel to the Tom's of Maine sale, TOMS founder Mycoskie retained ownership in his company (50 percent), as well as his title of "Chief Shoe Giver." As with the Tom's of Maine-Unilever commitment to environmental responsibility, Mycoskie said Bain promised to match his investment in a new fund to support socially minded entrepreneurship, and would continue the company's one-for-one policy.

Previous page, TOMS infographic sharing the TOMS story, from 2018 thank-you email sent to customers.

Great B2B storytelling

Because B2B companies frequently sell complex products or services, bringing their authentic stories to life can be more challenging. As we've discovered in Chapter 6, the 21st-century attention span of our audiences is shrinking. Great storytelling can break through the clutter if it's imaginative in its approach. Here are two great examples.

Corning: A day made of glass

In business communication, the most serious—and too frequently the most boring—specialty is investor relations. After all, it's about money, it's about stock, it's about the SEC and it's about lawyers. Get the picture?

Well, given the people and topics involved, most marketing to investors features no pictures—just words and numbers that blend together in tedium. This is why the video experiment by the glassmaker Corning and its business-to-business ad agency, Doremus, is so remarkable.

For a board of directors meeting, Corning engaged Doremus to produce a fascinating six-minute video story called "A Day Made of Glass." The video envisions a family interacting with glass as it will be in the future.

As so many good storytellers advise (including yours truly), Corning posted the beautiful video to YouTube. What happened next was magic.

Unlike most corporate videos posted to YouTube, which are categorically ignored, this one went completely viral. As I write, the video's had 26.8 million views. Once again, let's remember, this is a corporate video designed to show the investor value of Corning. Is anyone you know looking to view a video on that topic?

Why is it that it's impossible to be disengaged after viewing the Corning story depicted in this video?

It's not the technical details of the shoot. It's not the prowess of Doremus, a great agency. It's not even the imaginative uses of glass highlighted in the video.

The reason the video is compelling lies in the storytelling. By producing this video, Corning and Doremus intentionally tapped the most powerful medium in the world to tell a story. In most other hands, this presentation would be nothing more than tiny type and rivers of bullets in a War and Peace-length slide deck. In contrast, the video has no bullet points. There are no numbers to decipher. There are no lawyer-mandated disclosure statements. There's not even a single spoken word!

The video is a six-minute story about one day in the life of one family. Which is both surprising and obvious. After all, if Corning's future as a company is to have real financial value, it's going to have to create actual products used by real people in daily life.

That's what this video shows. Only the power of telling a story rooted in fact (imaginative riffs on current Corning products) and employing fluent storytellers (in this case an everyday family) could bring this story to life. This is the type of tangible storytelling that has driven the development of StoryCrafting at WordWrite.

Yes, storytelling is truly powerful. It can even kill the boring flavor that permeates far too much of investor relations. But don't take my word for it. View the video for yourself on YouTube—and see why 26.8 million viewers have already made the case for storytelling.

GE: An innovator celebrates innovators

For more than 18 months from 2011 to 2013, General Electric, one of the world's largest B2B companies, undertook an ambitious and unusual storytelling project to highlight its status as an innovator by sharing the stories of other remarkable innovators.

To achieve this objective, GE partnered with documentary filmmaker, Morgan Spurlock (*Super Size Me*) and engaged teams of documentary filmmakers to produce short films about leaders in medicine and other disciplines under the brand GE Focus Forward *Short Films, Big Ideas*.

GE launched the effort at the 2011 Toronto International Film Festival and shared 30 3-minute films at a number of other festivals around the world. In addition to the professionally produced films, the program included a user-generated film competition that drew more than 600 entries.

Twenty finalists were chosen from 69 countries. The winning film was called *The Cyborg Foundation*. It earned Spanish director Rafel Duran Torrent a $100,000 grand prize at the 2013 Sundance festival.

Torrent's film shares the story of Neil Harbisson, who was born with achromatopsia, a rare condition that left him color blind. In 2004, Harbisson and Adam Montandon developed the "eyeborg," a device that translates colors into sounds. Harbisson has turned his understanding of sound into a fascinating career as a painter and advocate for people interested in using technology to enhance their missing or diminished senses.

As *Fast Company* wrote when the GE series wrapped in 2013, "More than just a content-marketing gambit, the short documentaries ... were revelatory. From stories about breakthroughs in cancer testing and research to profiles of waste management and pollution pioneers, and break-through ideas in energy production, pain management, music creation and food access, the films give life to the people challenging convention and reimagining entrenched systems of belief."

GE's work in this project highlights a few critical aspects of storytelling and its power:

- Frequently, the best storyteller may not be the person at the top of the company's organizational chart—it may be someone who isn't even *on* the organizational chart. The heroes in the GE films make no mentions of GE and have no apparent association with the company, except that GE paid to bring their stories to life through film.

- Knowing your story archetype enables your organization to align itself with great story examples that may have nothing directly to do with what you make and sell. As GE's head of content development told *Fast Company*, the films are intended to "take people from being brand neutral or brand agnostic to brand advocates, because all of a sudden they saw GE associating themselves with these ideas that we believe in."

StoryCrafter's Toolkit
Chapter 7

If you're reading the printed edition of the book, access these links and resources through your web browser at: www.capitalsstory.com/storycrafterstoolkit.

If you're reading an electronic edition, just click the links in this box to access all the resources.

- Barry Schwartz, Paradox of Choice TED Talk
- A model, a dress and a great B2B story from GE
- The TOMS story, from the company website
- More on the Tom's of Maine story
- GE's Focus Forward film website

STORYTELLING AND SOCIAL MEDIA: MADE FOR EACH OTHER

At this point in our storytelling journey, we've explored nearly all the aspects of uncovering, developing and sharing your organization's great, untold story, which we've defined as your Capital S Story.

Here's an important aspect that deserves its own chapter: In the 21st century, it's impossible to conceive of any examination of successful storytelling without considering our digital world, especially social media.

For many organizations, the overwhelming volume and variety of social media seems to create one of the biggest storytelling roadblocks imaginable. In actuality, social media creates one of your organization's greatest opportunities to share your Capital S Story more broadly—and more successfully—than might have been possible even ten years ago.

In 1956, it took legendary filmmaker Cecil B. DeMille millions of dollars, a cast of thousands and the talents of Charlton Heston, Anne Baxter, Yul Brynner and many others to make his film *The Ten Commandments*, a masterpiece of cinematic storytelling that ranks among the top-ten highest grossing movies of all time.

Today, with a smartphone and access to the internet, your organization can adapt many of DeMille's classic storytelling techniques to your own Capital S Story. Think of it: not long ago, a fully immersive storytelling experience was possible only for moviemakers and those organizations that possessed enormous fortunes to bankroll those kinds of storytelling extravaganzas.

In the 21st century, social media and our digital world have leveled the playing field remarkably.

Let's consider just one social media platform for a minute— YouTube. If I asked you to name the most frequently used search engine on the internet, you'd likely answer Google, and you'd be right. If I asked you to name the second most frequently used search engine, you might struggle before realizing that it's YouTube. (And I'd forgive you if you didn't remember that YouTube is owned by Google.)

The democratization of social media, as represented by YouTube, is truly stunning. Consider these statistics about the world's largest video streaming and content service:

- The very first YouTube video was uploaded on April 23, 2005.
- The number of people who use YouTube is 1.3 *billion* and growing.
- More than 300 hours of video are uploaded to YouTube *every minute.*
- Nearly 5 billion videos are watched on YouTube every single day.
- YouTube gets more than 30 million visitors per day.
- In an average month, 8 of 10 people aged 18-49 watch YouTube.

As stunning as these statistics may be, they highlight the double-edged sword that so many organizations see when our firm starts working with them on social media storytelling for their great stories:

- The volume and variety of social media is frightening—often, it's paralyzing, because it's hard to know where to start and how to stand out.
- Yet, as the statistics also illustrate, whatever you or I may think about storytelling in the future, that future will largely be played out on social media.

So as we consider social media storytelling, let's start by acknowledging the challenges—and the opportunities—that social media presents. In this chapter, and in the accompanying sidebars, we'll provide additional context and fascinating examples of great storytelling employing social media.

WHAT COMES FIRST: A STORY OR SOCIAL MEDIA?

First, let's answer a fundamental question that ties back to our double-edged sword: Can you have great social media success without a great story? No. You might be able to do a one-day stunt of some type that generates a great deal of what we call "vanity metrics"—likes, clicks, retweets, etc. But without a great story, that one-day social media wonder will fade away and few will remember it even a week later.

You see, storytelling is not all about the fact that because of the technology, you can share whatever you are doing right now by tweet or Instagram or Facebook Live. No, storytelling is still all about storytelling.

If we were still dragging clubs and living in caves, we could still tell everyone who cared (and many who didn't) what we just ate for lunch without sending a tweet. It would just take a lot longer and be a heck of a lot less immediate, with much smaller reach.

So as great as social media can be in storytelling, a useful analogy is helpful first: Clean, fresh water has been a human need since the dawn of time. The same is true of successful storytelling. Societies, the record shows, need both to grow and thrive.

Yet when I examine conversations (online and otherwise) about the need for fresh water in sub-Saharan Africa, the debate is not about how cool the pipes are, how thick their walls are, the size of the pumping stations, water pressure, etc., etc. Sure, among a small community of companies and people who build pipes and water stations, that dialogue exists. Among those who need fresh water and those who hope to provide it? Nope. The conversation is about life-giving and life-saving water.

It's the same with storytelling. Great storytelling is about the content, not the pipes! So while social media is transformative in many ways, it's important to remember that all the platforms we know about today, and all those yet to be invented, are simply this: Tools. Yes, tools, just as the pipes that provide fresh water are not the life-giving liquid itself. Social media platforms are tools that enable storytelling, the life-giving narrative. They are not the life-giving narrative itself!

With the explosion of broad technological tools to communicate in the 21st century, it's never been more important to focus on the story you have to share, rather than getting lost in the pipes of how you share it.

Your story has never been more important, and while how you share it is an essential aspect of communication success, it's still about the content, not the pipes. Here's to drinking deeply from the pipes that deliver great stories.

SOCIAL STORIES WOULD MAKE DEMILLE PROUD

Once we grasp that the tools of social media storytelling far surpass what we might have had available to us even a few years ago, we begin to understand how we can more deftly tap that most powerful storytelling organ of all: Our brains.

In Chapter 2, we explored the history of our brains and why they crave stories. If you recall, it all begins with the very oldest part of our brains, that "reptilian" brain that we share with less-evolved creatures, the part of our brain that is responsible for responses to stimuli, such as flight or fight.

We recounted the work of Christophe Morin, co-author of the 2007 book *Neuromarketing* and a principal in the company SalesBrain, who identified six subconscious stimuli of the old brain:

1. **Self-Centered**: Is anything affecting your immediate survival?
2. **Contrasting**: Do you see a tiger in the tall grass ahead or is that merely a shadow?
3. **Visual**: Do you see a snake? OK, a snake can kill you! Move!
4. **Tangible**: Is this something you know, or if you don't, something that you can touch and evaluate?
5. **Emotional**: Do you see, hear or experience something that immediately stirs you to react by crying, laughing or engaging in some other emotional response without thinking about it?
6. **Self-Contained**: Do you detect a beginning and an end? In other words, is this a story, and can you follow it? Your attention span is short and so you'll pay attention to the beginning and perk up at the end.

Now let's lay our old brain's craving for stimuli against the storytelling characteristics that social media offers us:

- Because social media can offer a tailored experience, storytelling can focus on what immediately concerns you. For instance, your Facebook feed can be different than the feed offered to someone whose worldview is different.

- Social media thrives on contrast (differences of opinion, weird news, even disagreements about the color of a dress).
- Because social media is primarily visual, it taps into the old brain's needs deeply.
- Social media, because it lives on the internet, is not always tangible. That can be a challenge.
- But social media can be deeply emotional—and those emotions are real and tangible. When you see a sad video on Facebook or Twitter or YouTube or Instagram, your reactions are real. The tears are salty. The sadness creates real biological responses in your gut.
- And finally, because nearly every social media platform is defined by its constraints (length of posts, video length, etc.), social media provides a self-contained element of a beginning, middle and end.

Earlier in the book, we reviewed several examples of great modern storytelling that are also great examples of successful social media storytelling.

In Chapter 7, we looked at the powerful stories of Tom's of Maine and TOMS Shoes, two very different and socially conscious consumer businesses that have made their Capital S Story an essential ingredient in how they communicate with all of their audiences, largely on social media.

Also in Chapter 7, we looked at great storytelling from B2B companies. Corning Glass had great success with (of all things!) an investor relations video posted to YouTube, "A Day Made of Glass." General Electric infused its story into its program supporting filmmakers, the GE Focus Forward *Short Films, Big Idea* series.

We resurrect these examples for two reasons:

First, as their appearance throughout this book clearly illustrates, *social media storytelling is already a fact of life.* It's not a technique that's yet to be explored; it's well-established.

Second, at this point in our journey together—and with exposure to all the great social media storytelling success we just reviewed—I want to emphasize the importance of social media storytelling in sharing your own great untold story, regardless of whether you run a B2B or B2C organization.

To understand this better, let's take a look at another great social media storytelling success.

After 4 a.m. on the morning of Sunday, November 12, 2017, biologist Colin J. Carlson, Ph.D. gave up on his restless attempt to get a good night's sleep and did what so many others do in a similar situation: He turned to social media, specifically Twitter.

Unlike other Twitter aficionados whom you might name, Carlson's Twitter foray wasn't about ranting, raving, shaming or even saying things online that he might never say to someone in person.

No, Carlson's insomnia led him to share the complete story of the fox, one tweet burst at a time. And the Twitterverse, as it's called, "blew up" in response, making Carlson's insomniac experience a classic example of social media storytelling.

It began with this tweet:

Colin J Carlson
@ColinJCarlson

Replying to @ColinJCarlson
red fox (vulpes vulpes)
• the classic fox, the bar for foxness, a necessary prerequisite
• a good fox but NOT weird. weird-deficient. just a standard fox
• grade: B
4:18 AM · Nov 12, 2017

♡ 5,335 ◯ 784 people are talking about this

And with that, Carlson began to spin the foxy story that captured Twitter. It may have been Carlson's native talent or the storytelling genius buried deep in the core of all our old brains that we explored earlier in the book, or even simple insomnia, but Carlson then pivoted with a classic storytelling move: Distraction, creating a bit of suspense.

And from there, Carlson began spinning his very personal, subjective story of the fox—which captivated Twitter.

Colin J Carlson
@ColinJCarlson

Replying to @ColinJCarlson
tibetan sand fox (vulpes ferrilata)
• cubism is alive and well
• these eyes see into your soul
• a truly weird and unnerving fox design
• grade: A
4:22 AM · Nov 12, 2017

♡ 14K ◯ 4,080 people are talking about this

Colin J Carlson
@ColinJCarlson

Replying to @ColinJCarlson
Rüppell's fox (vulpes rueppellii)
• who authorized this transaction
• answers the question no one asked: what if a fox was made of spaghetti
• untrustworthy facial expressions
• potentially too deep in uncanny valley
• grade A-

4:25 AM - Nov 12, 2017

♡ 8,153   ♡ 1,875 people are talking about this

Carlson's storytelling caught the eye of everyday Twitter users and journalists, too—prompting stories by Mashable, Distractify and even *People* magazine, which summarized Carlson's work this way: "About 16 fox rankings later, Colin now has thousands of new followers and even more retweets, proving that if you take a fun, oddball approach to something furry, there is an audience out there to support you."

People's take on the content of Carlson's tweets is conventional social media wisdom. I would take issue with that interpretation: It's not just that social media (in this case, Twitter) likes furry animals, it's that great storytelling works, even in social media, and especially on a topic that is overrun with so much content.

I mean, don't even get me started on how many cat videos you can find on YouTube (more than 2 million, which have been viewed more than 25 billion times, apparently). The conventional wisdom is that if you do something goofy or eye-catching on social media, that's success. And it's not. At least, not the kind of success we want to have. Do you really believe that, if there are 2 million cat videos on YouTube, that whoever has viewed them 25 billion times can really tell them apart? Probably not, they are one-off parlor tricks, not true narratives. Carlson's tweets are different because they weave a narrative that goes beyond just one tweet or one hour of tweets.

Carlson's Twitter blasts on foxes illustrate that effective storytelling in social media (check out his language and the visual imagery it creates in support of the pictures he shared) can lift even a popular, oversaturated topic above the 21st-century digital clutter that faces all of us on a daily basis when trying to share our great, untold stories.

And this is the definition of storytelling success in social media—it's what we are seeking to share, our Capital S Story, with our best-fit clients.

Before his sleepless night, Carlson was a respected scientist with a focus on global climate change. Since November 12, 2017, Carlson's Twitter storytelling has expanded the reach and impact for his thinking by giving him a platform to show that he's a storyteller as well as a scientist.

Carlson's example illustrates that social media platforms are great tools for storytelling—if you have a good story to share and storytelling skills. Thus it has ever been when it comes to great storytelling. It's not about the pipes; it's about the content.

As with nearly every great thing in life, storytelling can be overdone, manipulated and misused. Such is the case with the popularity of the storytelling concept in marketing.

Before you embark on uncovering, developing and sharing your great untold story, you need to beware of the storytelling charlatans. We'll expose them in the next chapter.

When it's not real, is storytelling still authentic?

Chances are, you haven't met a storyteller like AREL. But someday soon, you will meet her—or someone (something?) like her.

AREL is not a person and in fact, it's my artistic license to presume that AREL is a "her." AREL is a computer-generated neural network that researchers at the University of California at Santa Barbara developed to construct complete stories from a series of images. Three times out of five, according to the research, AREL is a better storyteller than humans.

AREL is an acronym for Adversarial REward Learning (AREL) framework. AREL represents one of the most intriguing—and potentially challenging—developments in storytelling, the ability of machine learning to replace humans as storytellers.

This raises two very important questions for all of us who care about authentic storytelling: If a computer is making up a story, is it still authentic? And what happens if and when we reach a point at which computers tell better stories than humans? After all, we learned early on in this book that storytelling works because it's built into our human biology—we are hard-wired to share stories, remember them and live by them. Are we really on the precipice of a new era in which humans are no longer the best storytellers?

This is not some 1950s-era, science fiction fantasy. Artificial Intelligence, or AI, and its cousins, Augmented

---

Reality (AR) and Virtual Reality (VR) are already making themselves quite comfortable among us humans.

Hop on the internet to do some shopping and you will soon be exposed to all three. Whenever you visit an online shopping site and get a pop-up box that offers to help you with your shopping, you are experiencing AI. At this stage of the game, AI is most frequently the digitization of answers to the "most frequently asked questions" that you might have when shopping. Rather than waiting for a human to chat with you online or by phone, AI chatbots can do most of the work right now on simple questions—and they're getting better all the time.

Shopping online for a particular shirt or blouse? Want to see it on the model in a different color than you see when it first pops up in a picture? Click on the alternate color and now you're experiencing AR, reality that's been augmented to give you a sense of what something might look like as the model's shirt morphs from maize to lapis. Visit the mobile app stores for every flavor of smartphone operating system and you will find AR apps to help you picture what furniture might look like in your home, how to change color schemes in your wardrobe, etc., etc.

VR or virtual reality is more of an immersive experience. In pop culture (usually sophomoric beer commercials), it's young men wearing goggles stumbling around in the real world while chasing dragons in their VR goggles and flailing like zombies. But *real* VR is far more sophisticated than that. And its future is transformational.

As Forbes magazine put it in a 2017 article: "VR offers every business the chance to rethink how they present to and engage with their customers ... Rather than visit a physical showroom, customers leading increasingly digital lives will simply put on a headset and appear in a virtual one. Once there, they can interact with sales assistants—which could be virtual representations of real humans, or, more likely as time progresses, AI constructs operating independently of direct human control."

Depending upon how you feel about battling traffic or annoying sales clerks, this is all very enticing, or maybe a little challenging.

AI storytelling is a whole level beyond any of this. It's the replacement of the human mind in the creation of stories that we humans consume. And it's not that far off in the future, so we all better be ready for it.

And that brings us back to our friend AREL. The UC Santa Barbara researchers published a fascinating whitepaper on AREL's storytelling ability. I'll spare you the math so we can focus on the implications.

Not long ago, scientists learned that they could train machines to observe images (don't we all scan photos into our computers?) and by employing the complicated algorithms and repetitive learning capabilities of speedy computers, they could teach machines to see patterns and construct captions for pictures. When strung together, these pictures and captions could form the basis of a somewhat crude but cohesive story.

In reporting their work with AREL, the UC Santa Barbara researchers have crossed a new threshold: AREL successfully put together narratives that three times out of five, fooled test subjects who thought the narratives accompanying the pictures had been written by humans—you know, *real* storytellers.

Here is an example taken from the researchers' 2018 paper, *No Metrics Are Perfect: Adversarial Reward Learning for*

Visual Storytelling, published by the arXiv® service of Cornell University:

XF-ss	We took a trip to the mountains.	There were many different kinds of different kinds.	We had a great time.	He was a great time.	It was a beautiful day.
AREL	The family decided to take a trip to the countryside.	There were so many different kinds of things to see.	The family decided to go on a hike.	I had a great time.	At the end of the day, we were able to take a picture of the beautiful scenery.
Human-created Story	We went on a hike yesterday.	There were a lot of strange plants there.	I had a great time.	We drank a lot of water while we were hiking.	The view was spectacular.

In the reprinted example above, XE-ss is a previous version of AI storytelling. AREL is well, AREL, and you can see the bottom bar is the human-created story.

What does this mean for those of us committed to storytelling? In an article for the online publication, The Next Web, writer Tristan Greene put it this way:

"The implications for a storytelling AI are exciting. As developers figure out how to make the outputs generated by a neural network better align with human-thinking, we'll begin to see far-reaching advantages to plain language processors.

Sports referees, for example, could either be replaced or augmented with an AI capable of understanding and explaining a series of events. Do we really need to pay someone $188,322 to determine if Tom Brady is cheating or not?

It stands to reason that once AI is robust enough to explain its decision-making, by telling 'stories' about images in real-time, like 'Number 66, defense, offsides, the play results in a 5 yard penalty. Repeat first down,' we won't need people to do rules-based jobs that require an agent to do nothing more than observe and report.

And, let's not forget that there's an actual market for on-the-fly storytelling. If this technology ever fell into the hands of the developers at Telltale Games, or the designers at Wizards of the Coast (the company that makes Dungeons and Dragons), it could be used to generate a never-ending stream of unique, personal, entertainment."

It's too early in the AI storytelling journey to know with any certainty if the scenarios above will come to pass. It's not too early for those of us committed to storytelling to be thinking about how to separate the far reaches of computer-assisted storytelling from *real* storytelling.

Recall that early in the book we explored the definition of authenticity. While we didn't describe it this way in the earlier chapter, the concept of authenticity carries with it the presumption of a *lived experience*.

In our auto accident example in Chapter 4, we illustrated authenticity with a commonplace event that could happen to any of us, observing an auto accident from opposite sides of a crowded intersection.

In our example, two people witnessed the same event, but from different perspectives. One witness may tell the police one version of what happened based upon what he or she saw; another may have seen something else because of where he or she stood. Is one right and the other wrong? No. The two witnesses had different stories because of their perspective. In our definition, authenticity means that your great story reflects the views of all the participants—what they see, what they have to say, what they feel. This is what makes it unique.

What happens when you have a computer tooling around in the narrative *making stuff up*? What if the computer is constructing a narrative of something *that never happened*?

The arbiters of great fiction writing will probably have to decide whether computer-generated novels are better written than those constructed by humans at some not-too-distant future date.

For our purposes, we are focused on your Capital S Story. And that is a story that can only come from *lived experience*, a story that can't happen inside a computer processor, because it involves real events that shape and define real people and real organizations.

For us, it all comes back to biology. If thinking is uniquely human, then so is storytelling, because storytelling is the organization of thinking into rational narrative. The cognitive scientist Mark Turner put it this way: "Narrative imagining—story—is the fundamental instrument of thought. Rational capacities depend upon it. It is our chief means of looking into the future, or predicting, of planning, and of explaining."

What will machine storytelling bring us? Hard to say. But I take heart in my fundamental belief that to be human is to be a storyteller.

To quote Jonathan Gottschall, the author of *The Storytelling Animal: How Stories Make Us Human*, "The way we experience story will evolve, but as storytelling animals, we will no more give it up than start walking on all fours."

StoryCrafter's Toolkit
Chapter 8

If you're reading the printed edition of the book, access these links and resources through your web browser at: www.capitalsstory.com/storycrafterstoolkit.

If you're reading an electronic edition, just click the links in this box to access all the resources.

- Brilliant visual storytelling on Instagram
- 37 mind-blowing YouTube facts and figures
- Machine learning takes over in advertising
- The AREL study in PDF format
- CMOs need to think about marketing to robots
- Agency holding company Omnicom launches AI consultancy

9

BEWARE THE
STORYTELLING CHARLATANS

The problem with any good thing is that, sooner or later, people with bad motives try to claim it and twist it to their own ends. Usually, you can spot these snake oil salesmen. But maybe not without some help.

Almost as bad, people with seemingly respectable motives also try to cash in on the good thing, while not caring deeply about it. Think about all the companies that got rich selling supplies to miners during the 1800s California gold rush. Without breaking a sweat to pan for a single nugget, they happily sold supplies to many prospectors who had no idea what they were doing.

Sadly, both of these brands of charlatans have discovered storytelling.

The publication of this book comes about a dozen years after we first began working out the basic storytelling principles of what we now call StoryCrafting with our clients. Over that time, our commitment to storytelling has only grown stronger. Today, we better understand why it works, the importance of a Capital S Story and how an authentic story, fluently shared, can deliver results if you continually engage your audience.

Meanwhile, the prevalence of storytelling talk in the marketing field has gone from zero to unbelievable. No, literally, unbelievable. As in, "authors" and "experts" explaining that storytelling is how to lie to people to get them to do what they don't want to do. As in "experts" selling storytelling as the latest parlor trick while freely admitting they don't understand why it works but they're ready to teach you the tricks—for a hefty price. As in marketers who have no idea what storytelling is, but everyone else is using the word so they did a search and replace on all their marketing materials so they can use the word all the time too.

This is why LinkedIn, citing its historical data, can claim that there were zero marketing professionals in April 2011 claiming to be storytellers, yet by 2017, more than 570,000 claimed to be storytellers (see sidebar).

The purpose of this chapter is not to convince you that I'm the only person, or that my firm is the only organization, who can help you uncover and share your great, untold story. If you've read this far, you've made your own decision about the value of our thinking. My point is this: If you're going to invest your marketing dollars in storytelling, make sure you invest them with someone who's going to deliver the results you want.

The purpose of this chapter is to inject one last dose of storytelling vitamins so that no matter how you approach the sharing of your organization's great, untold story, you don't wind up sadly disappointed by some charlatan who doesn't have your best interests in mind.

Let's take a look at both categories of these storytelling charlatans in turn.

THE SNAKE OIL SALESMEN OF STORYTELLING

In today's world, it's not so hard to believe that big brands and experts you'd otherwise respect just plain lie when they share "authentic" stories.

One of the best-known examples of recent years is a brand whose name rides on the hoodies and sweatpants of teenagers across the world: the surf-associated clothing brand, Hollister.

In 2015, a blockbuster New Yorker article by Dave Eggers revealed that the entire story of the Hollister clothing company had been made up, probably in a corporate conference room at the Ohio headquarters of its parent company, Abercrombie & Fitch.

Even employees of the company were clueless that the origin story shared as the Capital S Story of Hollister was fake. As Eggers put it:

> For years, employees of Hollister stores, during orientation, were given the story, and it goes something like this: John M. Hollister was born at the end of the nineteenth century and spent his summers in Maine as a youth. He was an adventurous boy who loved to swim in the clear and cold waters there. He graduated from Yale in 1915 and, eschewing the cushy Manhattan life suggested for him, set sail for the Dutch East Indies, where he purchased a rubber plantation in 1917. He fell in love with a woman named Meta and bought a fifty-foot schooner. He and Meta sailed around the South Pacific, treasuring 'the works of the artisans that lived there,' and eventually settled in Los Angeles, in 1919. They had a child, John, Jr., and opened a shop in Laguna Beach that sold goods from the South Pacific—furniture, jewelry, linens and artifacts. When John, Jr. came of age and took over the business, he included surf clothing and gear. (He was an exceptional surfer himself.) His surf shop, which bore his name, grew in popularity until it became a globally recognized brand. The Hollister story is one of 'passion, youth and love of the sea,' evoking 'the harmony of romance, beauty, adventure.'

> None of this is true. Most of Abercrombie & Fitch's brands—including the now defunct Gilly Hicks and Ruehl No. 925—have had fictional backstories, conceived by Mike Jeffries, the company's former CEO.

Hollister was doing fine perpetrating its fake authentic story, coyly avoiding inquiries about whether the brand had anything to do with the real California coastal city of the same name. Of course, at the same time, what really riled the locals in Hollister, California, was that the brand's corporate attorneys tried to sue merchants there for selling goods that bore the name of the real city. In other words, a big corporation with a fake story was suing real people to stop them from sharing their real story, especially the name of their real city.

When confronted with its fakery, Abercrombie dissembled (a fancy word for lied some more) and a few of its spokespeople said things such as teenagers didn't really care that the story was fake. If you go back to Chapter 3, you will see that respected research demonstrates that this is patently untrue.

While fakery is apparently attractive, it is almost always unsuccessful in the end. For example, in Hollister's case, the CEO who concocted and "sold" the fake story of the company later departed because, despite all of his flimflam, the results were awful. He left the company after a series of several consecutive quarters of poor financial performance.

In other words, if you behave like the CEO of Hollister when it comes to sharing your story, it's going to catch up with you sooner or later.

Lest you think that Hollister's lying is an egregious example, rest assured that there is an entire industry of experts who find fakery in storytelling to be its ultimate best use.

And that includes marketing icon Seth Godin.

In our work, I talk about Godin quite a bit because he is among the top 10 or 20 recognized marketing "gurus" in the world. For more than 30 years, he's cultivated a very successful career of writing and speaking on marketing. With more than 20 books to his credit, Godin is also a prolific writer and hard worker. He is instantly recognizable even if you barely know him: His bald visage, usually accompanied by a colorful and stylish pair of glasses, peers from the front or back cover of most of his books. He has three talks currently on the respected TED Talks website.

Many in the marketing field swear by Godin. Once, for example, I attended a presentation where the speaker grumbled that many marketers must write lengthy blogs but Godin will often write merely a sentence "and it will be pure genius."

It may be genius but I fear it may also be built on a foundation of fakery—at least when it comes to story.

Among his many titles, the book that most sticks out for me is Godin's 2005 tome, *All Marketers Are Liars*. As you might suspect, the title alone is something of a truth-defying giveaway.

I find the book's entire premise to be a lie. Godin drew such criticism for how he originally wrote and marketed the book that he reissued it with a new title and foreword four years later.

For most of the book's length, Godin argues that all marketers use storytelling to lie to consumers to get them to buy things they don't need. In a chapter near the end, Godin makes a big reveal: Marketers aren't liars, they are truth tellers.

The "truths" marketers tell, according to Godin, are the lies that we tell ourselves. In other words, Godin argues that we as consumers lie to ourselves all the time about what we need. Marketers simply repeat the lies we tell ourselves to get us to buy the things we don't need but secretly want to fulfill our lie-filled fantasies. That, according to Godin, is a form of the truth.

This is a regrettable and manipulative approach to storytelling. I will give Godin his due: He is willing to put his name and face to what I find to be an insincere storytelling approach. Many others in the field hold the same views but are unwilling to own them publicly (the original dust jacket for *All Marketers Are Liars* had the usual Godin visage with a big Pinocchio nose strapped to his face).

If you've read this far into this book, you are probably as confused as I am that anyone—let alone a revered marketing guru—would twist the concept of authenticity to mean that your goal in sharing your story with your best-fit clients should be to tell them lies that you think they want to hear so they buy from you!

In 2009, Godin reissued the book with a new title, *All Marketers Tell Stories* (with the word Liars struck through and Tell Stories replacing it on the cover). Without acknowledging the criticism his original approach received, Godin tried to chart a slightly new path. For our purposes, these lines are most important:

"You believe things that aren't true. Let me say that a different way: many things that are true are true because you believe them."

This is the antithesis of authenticity as we've discovered it throughout this book. TV host and comedian Stephen Colbert has coined the word "truthiness" to describe this approach. When he first used the word on his Comedy Central show more than a decade ago, Colbert described it this way: "We're not talking about truth, we're talking about something that seems like truth—the truth we want to exist."

To me, that looks, sounds and feels like Godin's belief that "many things that are true are true because you believe them."

In previous chapters, we've addressed the issue of truth pretty directly. Early on, we looked at how different bystanders standing on different street corners could see the same accident and have different perspectives. But this is NOT what we're talking about here—shared human experiences may be experienced differently by people, but they are still grounded in reality.

If you really want to have success in sharing your Capital S Story, do you want to share the actual story or do you want your best-fit clients to interpret your story and believe what they want to believe, especially if what they wind up believing might turn out to be detrimental to your success? Do you really want to market to people who can't tell the difference between reality and fantasy? You know the answer to that question. Why would we settle for something less than our authentic story?

The second sentence in *All Marketers Tell Stories* that gives me heartburn is this:

"If what you're doing matters, really matters, then I hope you'll take the time to tell a story. A story that resonates and a story that can become true."

No Seth! Don't share a story "that CAN become true," share the story that IS true—the one that explains why someone should buy from you, work for you, invest in you, partner with you. Share your Capital S Story! Making up a story as you go along and hoping people buy into it is hardly authentic.

In fact, it reminds me of the Saturday Night Live sketch series that helped cement actor Jon Lovitz as a star of the 1990s SNL ensemble, when he played Tommy Flanagan (pronounced flan-A-gan), spokesperson of fictional Pathological Liars Anonymous. Poor Tommy couldn't help himself—to gain audience approval, once he started telling a story, he added whopper after whopper, punctuating each lie with a line Lovitz borrowed from actor Humphrey Bogart, "Yeah, that's the ticket!"

My favorite whopper? The time Lovitz appeared on the old Johnny Carson show and shared how a "flock of giant albino chickens" and "a small tidal wave" led to him founding Pathological Liars Anonymous.

Unless you want to become president of Pathological Liars Anonymous—stay away from the storytelling charlatans who assure you that we're all just lying to each other by telling stories, that the truth is not the truth, it's what we choose it to be.

Once you've taken your dose of storytelling vitamins, these storytelling charlatans are pretty easy to spot. What are these vitamins? Let's review:

- First, a commitment to authenticity, the knowledge that there are many sides to a story, and those sides *are still part of the same story;*
- Second, an understanding that to share your authentic story in ways that create results, you need fluent storytellers who are best able to reach your best-fit clients and engage them because of their personal characteristics as representatives of your Capital S Story;
- And finally, a commitment to continual audience engagement—to share your story again and again and ensure that it continues to deliver, you must be attuned to your audience so that your best-fit clients have a reason to continue engaging with you.

While the inauthentic charlatans are fairly easy to spot, it's the seemingly well-meaning storytelling charlatans that can fool you the worst. Let's look at why that's the case.

WHEN STORYTELLING IS "THE LATEST THING"

In four decades as a storyteller, I've met few people who don't like storytelling. As we learned earlier in the book, all of us have been storytellers and story consumers since our parents or other adults began reading to us when we were young.

So while most folks I meet like storytelling, they struggle to define it. The picture of a toddler snug in bed, drifting to sleep while *Goodnight Moon* or some other classic tale is read to them is a fairly universal experience. Beyond that, though, what is storytelling?

For far too many well-intentioned business leaders and marketers, it's just the latest thing. As I wrote earlier in this chapter, the well-intentioned "storytellers" who embrace the concept as the latest thing don't see storytelling as an elemental force of nature, the most primal of all means of human communication.

For these charlatans, storytelling is a tactic, like a card trick, that you slip into your marketing toolkit.

When you see an article proclaiming storytelling as the best thing ever to solve a very specific marketing problem, consider it a warning sign. For example, "5 Storytelling Tips to Make Your Marketing Videos More Interesting," on its face may seem innocuous, but think about it for a minute: It's not about your story; it's about your videos. Next year, if the same writers judge "story" to be a concept past its expiration date, they'll write something like "5 Camera Accessories to Make Your Marketing Videos More Interesting," and be just as happy.

There's nothing wrong with investigating, learning and applying a whole range of techniques to share your Capital S Story, including better video techniques. My point is this: For far too many marketers, story is just a low-level, flavor of the month gimmick. For them, it doesn't rise to the level of importance that we've come to understand on our journey together. And if you work with these storytelling charlatans, it's pretty certain you'll be shortchanged by the results.

For "storytellers" in this second category, storytelling is a concept that gets clients to sign on the bottom line, enabling agencies or marketing teams to do what they've always done while calling it "storytelling."

When you see or hear phrases such as, "Learn how to use story to frame any disruptive message," you can see quickly that the commitment to story is fairly thin, even if the company has "story" in its name (which the company in this example does).

The test is this: Can you replace the word "story" in what the company is promising with some other term and not see an appreciable difference? If you replaced the word "story" in the sentence above with the phrase "strategic marketing" or the word "psychology" or some other variation—how much difference would it make? Not much.

Yet another example—one company does an annual event supposedly about storytelling that describes itself as "TED for creatives." The description of what participants receive from attending goes like this: "regroup and redefine your process as you set out to push past your organizational goals." Huh? What specifically does that have to do with storytelling?

If you've read this deeply into this book, you probably want more than a storytelling card trick. You want more than the same old classic advertising that doesn't work, and that won't work any better just because you call it "storytelling." You understand that your Capital S Story is your most powerful marketing asset—and you want to make the best use of it!

So what to do then, when you are confronted by those who readily agree that storytelling is cool but see it more as a means to an end rather than an end in itself?

First, stick to your storytelling principles. If you believe in your Capital S Story, fight for it by committing to work with someone who'll respect your Capital S Story, empower your fluent storytellers and make sure your story connects with the audiences you most need to reach.

Second, accept that authentic stories must be shared by fluent storytellers.

Third, continually read your audience to make sure they're engaged and work with those who are willing to adapt their approaches to deliver your best-fit clients.

Finally, inspire yourself by seeing how some of the greatest corporate storytellers do it. And that will be our last stop on our journey before you head out to uncover, develop and share your own great, untold story. Get ready to learn about EKINs!

Authenticity: What's old is seemingly new

Unless you're a marketing geek, you've probably never heard of James Gilmore and Joseph Pine II. They aren't New York celebrities; their consultancy, Strategic Horizons, operates out of the Cleveland suburb of Aurora, Ohio.

You may not have heard of Gilmore and Pine, but I'll bet you know the concept that put them on the map, *The Experience Economy*. That's the title of just one of their several books, and the name for a set of guiding principles that encourages companies to focus on creating memorable experiences for those who buy their products or services if they hope to create deep and lasting connections and loyalties.

As they deepened their definition of the experience economy, Gilmore and Pine wrote a book called *Authenticity*, which urged companies to "grasp, manage, and excel at rendering an authentic experience" to win in the marketplace. *Authenticity* first hit shelves in 2008 and its basic premise is as fresh today as it was then—and decidedly more topical in an era of "fake news."

When Donald J. Trump became president in 2016, the debate over the meaning of authenticity took on added emphasis. Our focus is not on the added emphasis or on politics.

For our purposes, the original publication of *Authenticity* and its endurance in the decade since demonstrate the central importance of authenticity in sharing your Capital S Story with your best-fit clients, especially in a market-place of ideas that's now been shaped by the intense heat of debate over its meaning.

Because their prescient assessment of the value of authenticity came long before more recent political wars over the term and its meaning, it's worth revisiting some of the key principles Gilmore and Pine laid out, and assessing them in light of what we know to be true about the importance of authenticity in sharing your Capital S Story with your best-fit clients.

For Gilmore and Pine, authenticity means:

- Finding experiences between consumers and companies that step outside our "digital first" 21st-century environment. In other words, much of what we do today is done online, but what makes it real? Gilmore and Pine contend that answering that question is critical for companies committed to authenticity.
- They also argue that companies must give their customers experiences that "reflect who they are and who they aspire to be in relation to how they perceive the world—with lightning-quick judgments of 'real' or 'fake' hanging in the balance. "
- Sadly though, Gilmore and Pine contend that not all companies can be transparent and authentic and they create an approach to authenticity they call

"fake-real." Just reading those two words together give me pause (and I hope you as well). In applying the concept of your Capital S Story—there can be no "fake-real" alignment. Your Capital S Story provides the honest answers to why someone would buy from you, work for you, invest in you or partner with you. None of those relationships can be "fake real" if they are to deliver results, or if they are to last.

What then do we learn from Gilmore and Pine, two consultants who've predicted some important marketing trends? Authenticity never goes out of style. And sadly, neither does the temptation to fake it!

How do I overwhelm thee?
Let me count thy storytellers

Just how many storytellers are there anyway, and what defines a storyteller?

In a 2018 issue of its marketing magazine devoted to story-telling, the professional social network LinkedIn tried to answer this question. In an article called The Rise of Story-telling, LinkedIn used its historical data pulled from professional profiles over the years, and some subjective interpretation, to determine just what makes a storyteller anyway.

For LinkedIn, of course, the answer has a lot to do with what people call themselves. The LinkedIn survey of its data sought the keyword "storyteller" in profiles as the key measure of the rise of storytelling. According to LinkedIn, in 2011, no marketer on the social network had the keyword "storyteller" in their profile (I find this a bit hard to believe since I was on LinkedIn back then with my current title, president and chief storyteller at WordWrite).

Regardless, the LinkedIn data does illustrate one somewhat useful measure of what it means to be a practicing storyteller in the marketing realm: Do marketers include "storytelling" in their profiles.

According to LinkedIn, the sea change for storytelling in marketing came in a period "from August 2011 to August 2012 that created unstoppable momentum behind this form of content and its role in brand relationships."

While I'm skeptical that the simple act of putting the word "storyteller" into your LinkedIn profile tells us a great deal about the value of storytelling in sharing your authentic story with your best-fit clients, the social network data does give us some interesting perspective. For example:

- Over a five-year period from 2012 to 2017, the number of LinkedIn profiles with storytelling listed as a skill or title rose from 5,000 to 570,000.
- LinkedIn credits a few marketing campaigns, books and marketing gurus for the rise: Seth Godin, Gary Vaynerchuk of Vayner Media, Coca-Cola and Chipotle's inventive "Food with Integrity" campaign and its centerpiece Scarecrow video and video game.
- LinkedIn predicts that virtual reality and communities of storytellers such as The Future of StoryTelling (FoST) will drive what's next in storytelling in marketing.

I suppose to adequately make such a prediction about the future, LinkedIn needs to be looking at profiles again for the keywords "virtual reality" in some proximity to "storytelling" and for profiles mentioning membership in storyteller communities such as FoST.

Until LinkedIn can credibly tie the appearance of keywords in social network profiles to actual competency in sharing your Capital S Story with your best-fit clients, the data is entertaining and interesting but no measure of how many effective storytellers exist in the marketing realm.

StoryCrafter's Toolkit
Chapter 9

If you're reading the printed edition of the book, access these links and resources through your web browser at: www.capitalsstory.com/storycrafterstoolkit.

If you're reading an electronic edition, just click the links in this box to access all the resources.

- Seth Godin on controversy over his book title
- Seth Godin on changing his book title
- Synthetic authenticity from Time Magazine
- The four lies of storytelling
- The history of truthiness from Wikipedia
- The real history of 'fake news'

10

JUST DO IT:
YOUR CAPITAL S STORY
CAN DRIVE YOUR SUCCESS

Mention the name Nike and for most people, a montage of images comes to mind: Michael Jordan leaping to the bucket aboard his Air Jordans; Tiger Woods assessing the cut of the green as he cups his hands over his Nike Golf visor; maybe even Mick Jagger or another celebrity out on the town in their Nike kicks.

Listen to those willing to pay twice as much for a keychain with the Nike swoosh on it as the one that hangs next to it in a convenience store, naked of the famous symbol, and you'll hear what might be a near-religious description of why the swoosh on it is worth more than the same item without the logo.

Enter a Niketown store, and dive into an experience that is the marriage of athletics, performance, innovation and cool that creates an indescribable, unmistakable and seductively attractive vibe. Most people who step into a Nike store will never be the world's best at any athletic endeavor. Yet by connecting with the company, they can be part of the same tribe that wins gold medals and NBA championships and the Masters at Augusta.

What is it about a company that's been "in" for most of its 50 years that delivers this full-sensory experience? Many experts would tell you it's the brand. They would probably point to the swoosh, or the star athletes or the hip, subtly anti-authority sensibility of the company.

Most experts would be wrong—what they see, hear and experience in all of these wonderful representations of Nike may, in some ways, be the Nike brand. But more importantly, they are manifestations of the Nike story, which drives the brand because the brand derives from the story. And without that story, the brand is just not the same.

No company in 21st-century business better represents the full package of culture, science, biology and organizational commitment that brings storytelling to the forefront of success than Nike. Nike's story not only sells shoes, it motivates employees, it attracts athletes, and it engages audiences far beyond the mid-1960s track meets where it all began with hardcore runners committed to running at a time before running was cool.

To understand the Nike story, we have to go back to that track at Hayward Field at the University of Oregon. Most who know the Nike story expect to find Phil Knight on that track. The leader of Nike for most of its history, Knight was indeed a runner and certainly ran that track as a miler. Later, he would become the company's co-founder and one of its most fluent storytellers.

But in the beginning, as with Southwest Airlines, there was another hero present at the creation.

In speaking about storytelling across the country, I frequently ask audiences to name the founder of Nike. Phil Knight is the most common answer. Rarely (if at all) does even a single person mention his co-founder, Bill Bowerman. This is surprising, since, aside from co-founding Nike, Bowerman was a great track coach, with 31 Olympic athletes, 51 All-Americans, 12 American record-holders, 24 NCAA champions and 16 sub-4 minute milers to his credit. In 24 years coaching at the University of Oregon, his track and field team had a winning season every season but one and earned 4 NCAA titles.

To understand the story of Nike, we have to understand the story of Bill Bowerman. Before Nike, there was Phil Knight and Geoff Hollister and other runners who later became the company's first employees. But there was only one coach, and that was Bowerman.

Bowerman wasn't after the creation of an iconic company or brand in the beginning; he just wanted better equipment for his runners and he was frustrated by the thought that major sporting goods makers gave to running as a sport, which is to say, no thought at all.

Running attire wasn't good enough, so he fashioned a lighter gear from parachute material probably much like he saw frequently during his time as a leader of the Army's 10th Mountain Division in Italy during World War II.

Cutting parachutes into running shorts was one thing; figuring out how to replace the clunky shoes that wore out quickly and frequently injured his runners was more difficult. At one point, Bowerman, a tinkerer and innovator, tried using the family's waffle iron as a mold for shoe soles that would better cushion runners' feet while they ran. He ruined the waffle iron but started the thinking on what would later become some of the company's most iconic designs from its early years.

Bowerman was more than a tinkerer, he was a thinker and a leader, an iconic figure whose motivational skills ran the gamut from the bawdy (urinating on his runners at one point) to the sublime, emphasizing a 'team first' commitment to athletic excellence that meant every runner on the team was important to the overall achievements of the team, not just the guy who took first place. Decades later, the spirit and the lessons Bowerman taught continue to infuse Nike culture.

As is the case with most track and field athletes, Bowerman's runners went on to other pursuits when their collegiate careers were over. For Phil Knight, the next career step was Stanford Graduate School of Business. It was there that inspiration struck and the idea blossomed that Bowerman's tinkering and innovating should be more than a small endeavor. Knight saw a company with a mission and passion to take Bowerman's values and ideas to runners everywhere.

He visited his coach in 1964 and on a handshake deal, they started Blue Ribbon Sports, which would later become Nike. Knight handled the business end of things, Bowerman was Bowerman. In the early years, more and more of Bowerman's runners joined the company. They already knew the story and they immediately shared a culture and camaraderie. It was a mixture of a commitment to excellence and an anti-authority bent that might have started with huge skepticism of the poor running shoes made by major sporting goods companies, but which was burnished and polished into a general attitude and approach to the work that propelled the company's growth.

Working at Nike was different because of this than working at any other sporting goods company. It wasn't just the authenticity of the work, or the leadership of fluent storytellers such as Knight or Bowerman, it was the commitment to deliver to the running community what runners wanted. This meant, as other writers have put it, not only committing to storytelling to explain what Nike was all about, but also committing to story listening, which meant Bowerman, Knight and others would begin the product development process by talking with runners, visiting tracks, seeing their challenges and sharing their experiences.

In the early years of the company, champion runner Steve Prefontaine, who was coached by Bowerman at Oregon, became the most important audience that the Nike team would meet with again and again, engaging him to see if they had met his exacting standards with new designs. A harsh and demanding critic, Prefontaine was one of the best middle distance runners in the world and helped popularize running as a leisure activity in the 1970s. His tragic death in an auto accident at age 24, several months before he expected to compete in the 1976 Olympics, added to the aura and mystique around him, and by extension, Bowerman and Nike.

Nike itself was a huge promoter and beneficiary of the 1970s running boom. By 1980, the company enjoyed a 50 percent market share in the United States and had quadrupled in size. As Nike grew, it became clear that it would soon run out of all the available, capable former University of Oregon runners who already knew the Bowerman philosophy and story. So early on in its history, Nike began storytelling sessions for new employees because working at Nike was different than working at other sporting goods companies, and the mission was bigger. It was important that new employees understand right from the beginning that they weren't just there to make and sell shoes; they were there to help athletes (and everybody who wanted the same gear as athletes) to buy and use the best equipment it was possible to create.

Over time, the storytelling sessions expanded to two full days during orientation. While beginning with a history of the company, the sessions included the stories of leaders in the company, many of them who knew Bowerman or had joined early in the company's history, to gain the context and meaning of Nike. This process imbeds the concept of storytelling into the work life DNA of new Nike employees even before they can find their way to the restroom. Including storytelling at the front end of the employee experience elevates the importance of the company's story and ingrains values, behaviors and beliefs in ways that we know human biology and culture encourage.

As leaders share their Nike stories, they provide archetypes of several storylines that the new employees are likely to encounter during their careers by connecting the new employees to stories that explain the humble, striving roots of what is today one of the world's best-known companies.

Given what we've discussed earlier in the book, it's easy to see how these stories become the pathways or maps by which Nike employees can expect to navigate the days, months and years ahead in situations in which they will be called upon to be representatives of the overall Nike story.

This kind of orientation is a far cry from the typical corporate welcome videos or the deluge of paperwork that dominate so many corporate orientation programs. I'm sure new Nike employees have to fill out plenty of required paperwork. I'm also sure that the storytelling component of their orientation makes a far more dominant and lasting impression on their careers, and their success at Nike.

The importance of sharing the Nike story took on additional dimensions outside the workforce as the company grew and its potential customer audiences extended far beyond the relatively small circle of competitive runners or those who ran for leisure. Even though Nike entered soccer and other sports early, the same focus on the athlete that is so central to its story had to be explained to those outside the top tiers of competitive sports.

To spread the Nike story while selling shoes and sporting goods to those who didn't know why the company and its products were different and better, the company began an intensive boot camp experience for its technical sales force. As the tech group grew, it took on more and more of a distinct personality within the company. Among other attributes, the techs began calling themselves Ekins, for Nike spelled backwards. The name stuck. And they literally began branding themselves, beginning a boot camp graduation ritual in which Ekins got ankle or leg tattoos of the Nike swoosh.

More important than these symbols of achievement was the full, sensory experience of the Ekins course, which unlike the other aspects of the Ekins subculture, was intentionally designed by the company with the goal of infusing the Nike story into this important group of company ambassadors, who would be expected to share that story on a daily basis.

On the first day of the nine-day Ekins boot camp, participants are taken to the Hayward Field track where Bowerman coached, to stand where he did and to run where his champions ran, to drink in the full experience of where and why Nike began. The Ekins also visit the site where Prefontaine died and view a movie about his life. These experiences are intended to be both meaningful and memorable, to provide the context and perspective that illustrate that Nike is certainly about selling shoes and sporting goods but it's about much more than that.

In addition to exposing Ekins to the authenticity of the Nike story and turning them into fluent storytellers, the experience also prepares them to become great listeners, just as Knight and other early employees were great listeners. Working with retail store employees, customers, athletes and others, Ekins are expected to listen to the market and bring back to the company what they have learned.

Storytelling at companies that understand how their story lives in a place above and beyond the brand is not just about orientation or subcultures of unusual storytellers. It's about making the story part of everyday corporate life.

At Nike, this is accomplished by designating a chief storyteller. By empowering Nelson Farris, at this writing the Nike employee with the longest tenure, as its chief storyteller, the company puts into action the concept that great organizations can only understand their future by understanding their past. Farris, given his more than 40 years at the company, is the connective tissue and resident oracle who can link today's Nike back to the days of Bowerman.

Officially, Farris is responsible for Global HR Talent Development. Unofficially, he is the collective memory of the organization. He is the touchstone by which the future course of the company, on matters big and small, can be measured. He is the keeper of the flame, or in this case, the swoosh. His role in the company is acknowledged regularly in numerous ways—he speaks at corporate events, blogs, trains and in other ways makes sure that the Nike story is at the forefront of what the company is doing.

An authentic story shared by fluent storytellers and continuous reading of the audience—the three critical elements of successful business storytelling are alive at Nike. And the company has added to its practice of storytelling by institutionalizing a role for the keeper of the story in Nelson Farris.

You may say, reading this book, that your company is no Nike. And I would say you are right. You might look around and conclude that there is no Bill Bowerman or Phil Knight in your organization. And I would say you are right. And you might add, for emphasis, that you can't conceive of having a Nelson Farris on staff. And again, I would say you are right.

And then I would congratulate you for understanding that Nike's story is Nike's story and you shouldn't be trying to tell Nike's story.

I would then remind you that while your organization's story is not Nike's story, it is certainly its own story and it's worth sharing. And I would remind you that the same biology, culture and history that makes storytelling a success at the great companies we admire—Southwest, Nike and others we've examined in this book—guide your story as well.

In the end, each of us as business leaders must ask the same questions:

- What is our authentic story?
- Who is best equipped to share it?
- And how will we, as an organization, ensure that our story is always relevant to the audiences we must reach?

These are the fundamental questions that will guide you as you infuse storytelling into your marketing. They are the essential ingredients that enable you to develop storylines based upon classic archetypes that shortcut the information-cluttered marketing that bombards all of us in the 21st century.

Understanding and sharing your story will enable you to make the best strategic decisions about your marketing because you will be focused on your story and who needs to see, hear and experience it, rather than focusing the bulk of your energy (and financial resources) on tactical decisions such as the color of your brochure (if you even need a brochure).

At WordWrite, it's been our mission to bring together our hard-earned experience with storytelling and our understanding of strategic communications to create a complete process that delivers measurable results. With StoryCrafting, we have focused on what matters most: creating dialogue, conversations and relationships that deliver lasting value. By focusing our efforts on a process that transcends time, culture and society, we are tapping a communication force that works just as well on Twitter as it did on tablets (and by that I mean the ones chiseled from stone). To lay the groundwork for our unique approach to storytelling, we have had to understand storytelling from the bottom up and from beginning to end.

Why does your story drive your brand? Because before you had a brand, you had a story. Before you had a product or service to sell, you had a story. Before you hired your first employee, made your first million, hit whatever first milestone is important to you and your business, you had a dream and a passion and a vision. And you told whoever would listen over and over and over again the story of your dream, painting a picture, hitting the right notes and creating an infectious feeling about your vision that had others tagging along and signing up.

This essential story creation, shaping and sharing is hard-wired into our biology. We have the science today to prove it. Storytelling's success is also reinforced by thousands of years of culture, history and practice. It is the same whether you are an entrepreneur, a new head of marketing in a start-up, the CEO of a fast-growing gazelle, a Fortune 50 behemoth or a crusading non-profit.

So I leave you with this challenge: Uncover your Capital S Story, find your fluent storytellers and start sharing. As you share your great story with the audiences you need to reach, continually engage them to ensure they're part of that story.

May you always be the hero in your own story, and may the power of storytelling deliver you happy endings again and again and again.

StoryCrafter's Toolkit
Chapter 10

If you're reading the printed edition of the book, access these links and resources through your web browser at: www.capitalsstory.com/storycrafterstoolkit.

If you're reading an electronic edition, just click the links in this box to access all the resources.

- Memoirs of an EKIN, Nike's coolest job
- Nike's story through the eyes of its #3 employee
- How Siemens uses storytelling with clients, staff
- The Nike Story? Just Tell It!
- Telling Tales: The Art of Corporate Storytelling
- Bill Bowerman: Nike's Original Innovator

# # #

ABOUT THE AUTHOR

Paul Furiga is president and chief storyteller of WordWrite. Founded in 2002, WordWrite is a perennial top-ranked firm. In O'Dwyer's national rankings, WordWrite posted the fourth-greatest growth among 123 ranked agencies in 2017. In 2019, the *Pittsburgh Business Times* named WordWrite one of the 50 fastest growing companies in Western Pennsylvania.

Paul has been honored by the Pittsburgh chapter of the Public Relations Society of America (PRSA) with its Renaissance Hall of Fame Award. The chapter's highest honor recognizes a professional who's made a substantial impact in the region.

WordWrite has received numerous awards for its work, from PRSA, IABC and other professional organizations. Its work has also appeared in PR News books as case studies of excellence.

Paul's passion for storytelling inspired him to form WordWrite and to focus on developing the concept of a Capital S Story, the story above all others that explains why someone would buy from an organization, partner with it, invest in it or work for it.

Before founding WordWrite, Paul was a vice president at Ketchum Public Relations, where he served clients including Alcoa, Bridgestone/Firestone and Rutgers University.

Paul also spent two decades as a journalist. He edited the *Pittsburgh Business Times*, was an editor and correspondent for the Thomson Washington, D.C. bureau, and was senior editor of OhioWeek and a reporter for The Cincinnati Enquirer.

As a Congressional Fellow of the American Political Science Association, Paul was an aide to U.S. Sen. Paul Simon of Illinois and later, issues director for Simon's 1988 presidential run. Paul graduated from Miami University in Ohio in 1980 with a degree in mass communication.

HOW TO WORK WITH WORDWRITE

For two decades, story has infused everything we do at WordWrite. Our collaboration with clients has taught us that a Capital S Story that's successfully uncovered, developed and shared creates the best branding possible.

We're passionate about storytelling and committed to being honest brokers of communication. Our clients' success since 2002 proves that the power of authentic, well-developed stories moves hearts and minds and delivers results.

We're explorers. We seek to learn—about our clients, their challenges, their successes. We're excited about what our clients do and are driven to deliver results. We have an insatiable hunger to question the boundaries of what we know, and as we challenge those limits, we provide benefits to our clients and to society.

Why story? Because before you had a brand, you had a story. Before you had an idea or product or service, you had a story. Before you hired your first employee, made your first million, hit whatever first milestone matters to you and your organization, you had a dream, a passion—a vision. And you told whoever would listen over and over and over again the story of your dream, painting a picture, hitting the right notes and creating an infectious feeling that had others tagging along and signing up.

Let our storytelling team help you explore the next chapter in your great, untold story.

At WordWrite, we've successfully guided hundreds of clients to uncover, develop and share their great, untold story—their Capital S Story—through our story-infused process. Explore our website, then contact us to learn how WordWrite can help your organization achieve the greatest possible success by sharing the story that matters above all others, your Capital S Story.

To contact author Paul Furiga, visit

Website:	www.wordwritepr.com
Email:	paul.furiga@wordwritepr.com
LinkedIn:	https://www.linkedin.com/in/paulfuriga/ https://www.linkedin.com/company/ wordwrite-communications/
Twitter:	https://twitter.com/paulfuriga https://twitter.com/wordwritepr/
Facebook:	https://www.facebook.com/wordwritepr/
Instagram:	https://www.instagram.com/wordwritepr/